Who is *Not* Poor? Dreaming of a World Truly Free of Poverty

Lant Pritchett

When the World Bank dreams of "a world free of poverty," what should it be dreaming? In measuring global income or consumption expenditure poverty, the World Bank has widely adopted the $1 a day standard as a lower bound. Because this standard is based on poverty lines in the poorest countries, anyone with income or expenditures below this line will truly be poor. But there is no consensus standard for the upper bound of the global poverty line: above what level of income or expenditures is someone truly not poor? This article proposes that the World Bank compute its lower and upper bounds in a methodologically equivalent way, using the poverty lines of the poorest countries for the lower bound and the poverty lines of the richest countries for the upper bound. The resulting upper bound global poverty line would be 10 times higher than the current lower bound and at least 5 times higher than the currently used alternative lower bound of $2 a day. And in tracking progress toward a world free of poverty, the World Bank should compute measures of global poverty using a variety of weights on the depth and intensity of poverty for a range of poverty lines between the global lower and upper bounds. For instance, rather than trying to artificially force the global population of 6.2 billion (a billion is 1,000 million) into just two categories "poor" and "not poor," with the new range of poverty lines the estimates would be that 1.3 billion people are "destitute" (below $1 a day), another 1.6 billion are in "extreme poverty" (above $1 a day but below $2 dollar a day), and another 2.5 billion are in "global poverty" (above extreme poverty but below the upper bound poverty line).

Poverty reduction is the objective of the World Bank, and poverty measured by income or expenditure is one key dimension of poverty. In the standard measures of poverty reduction, the income gains of people above the poverty line count for nothing. The highest poverty line ever officially used to measure and track global poverty is $2 a day,[1] and by that standard 3.25 billion people are *not poor*. The unavoidable conclusion is that the income gains of 3.25 billion people count for nothing in the World Bank's objective of income poverty reduction. One would think that before

doi:10.1093/wbro/lkj002   Advance Access publication 25 January 2006   21:1–23 telling 3.25 billion people that their economic progress means nothing to your organization, you would have a firm analytical, empirical, or normative foundation. But that is not the case. There is no justification for using $2 a day as an upper bound global poverty line (GPL^{UB}) to define who is not poor.

Since the very notion of poverty is a social construct, any poverty line used as a particular empirical measure of poverty is also a social convention.[2] The appropriate range of poverty lines therefore depends on social context—who is setting the line, whose poverty is being measured, and to what purposes the lines are being put. Social acceptability, policy relevance, and spatial and intertemporal comparability are key criteria in establishing a poverty line in a particular context. The World Bank uses hundreds of different poverty lines in its dialogue with countries about their policies. It does not, and should not, impose an external standard for poverty lines. Similarly, nothing in this article addresses the setting of national poverty lines. But when the World Bank as an organization says that it "dreams of a world free of poverty," it should have its own definitions of *global* poverty against which to gauge progress toward that dream.

The World Bank should measure global income or expenditure poverty using a range of global poverty lines, with sets of intensity weights (discussed below) for each. A range needs a lower bound and an upper bound. The $1 a day standard deserves its wide acceptance as the lower bound global poverty line (GPL^{LB}): people below this line are indisputably poor. But a debate of how to set the upper bound for a global poverty line has been missing. The method for setting the standard for who is not poor has been entirely ignored.

The method for setting a GPL^{UB} proposed here results in a $10 a day standard—10 times higher than the current lower bound of $1 a day and 5 times higher than the de facto upper bound of $2 a day. The article defends this upper bound on grounds of methodological consistency, economic soundness, and as a better reflection of the World Bank's true poverty objective than a low upper bound. At this higher poverty line, the headcount rate of global poverty is roughly 40 percentage points higher—bringing 2.5 billion people into the definition of the "global poor" and so into the ambit of the World Bank's concern with poverty reduction.

Objectives and Poverty Lines

How does one choose between the economists' usual normative objective for policy analysis, improving a social welfare function, and poverty reduction as the objective? Whereas some economists argue that income gains should be counted equally at all levels, in practice nearly all social welfare functions are "inequality averse" and count gains to the poor more. The real difference between a social welfare and a poverty approach is that a poverty-reduction objective counts gains to the nonpoor less—infinitely less in fact. Because a large class of both social welfare functions and poverty measures can be thought of as weighted integrals over income distributions and the mathematical form of a social welfare function can be quite flexible in how much concern is given to the poor, the only essential difference between the two is that poverty lines imply a level of income above which gains to income count for exactly zero. This is the essential difference because any combination of a poverty measure and a social welfare function is just another social welfare function. Thus, the only feature of a poverty measure that a social welfare function cannot represent is a zero weight above the poverty line.

Even among development economists, a poverty-reduction objective as an appropriate normative ordering for policy analysis is not widely embraced. As usual, Angus Deaton (1998a, p. 141) gives a succinct and accurate summary:

> For policy evaluation, the social welfare function is all that is required to measure welfare, including an appropriate treatment of poverty. While it is possible—and in my view desirable—to give greater weight to the needs of the poorest, I see few advantages in trying to set a sharp line, below which people count and above which they do not. Poverty lines and poverty counts make good headlines, and are an inevitable part of the policy debate, but they should not be used in policy evaluation. Perhaps the best poverty line is an infinite one; everyone is poor, but some a good deal more so that others, and the poorer they are the greater weight they should get in measuring welfare and in policy evaluation.

The reason why nearly all economists prefer the social welfare function over the poverty-reduction objective as the normative ordering for policy evaluation can be illustrated with five examples. Three examples show that the poverty-reduction objective is too often indifferent, and two examples show that it is too extreme. First, imagine a policy that raises the income of all individuals above the poverty line, while leaving the income of those below the poverty line unchanged. This new policy set is preferred by nearly any social welfare function, but a poverty-reduction objective ranks the two the same. Second, suppose that the very rich could be taxed at little welfare cost and the proceeds transferred to those just above the poverty line. This is again a preferred normative outcome for any sufficiently inequality-averse social welfare function but an indifferent one for a poverty-reduction objective. Third, change the framing by supposing that a policy created restrictions on competition that allowed the very rich to charge higher prices for a good consumed by the almost poor but not by the poor, transferring income from the almost poor to the rich. Even assuming away the inefficiency, any sufficiently inequality-averse social welfare function would rate this policy a loser, but a poverty-reduction objective still has no preference—it remains stubbornly indifferent to all changes above the poverty line.

Economists are averse to a poverty-reduction objective as a normative ordering not only because it too frequently lacks a preference but also because its preferences are too extreme when it has them. The fourth example concerns a tax-transfer scheme in which taxes on those above the poverty line are levied at rate $\tau(y - PL)$, but for whatever reason, a fraction δ of the amount raised disappears, and only $(1 - \delta)\tau(y - PL)$ is received by those below the poverty line. Even if δ is very near one so that the transfer is enormously inefficient, a poverty-reduction objective would prefer the transfer. So if $1 million were taxed from those above the poverty line, $999,999 were deposited into someone's Swiss bank account, and $1 were transferred to the poor, a poverty-reduction objective would favor this policy. The fifth example is the converse. Suppose there was a very efficient scheme for taxing all incomes in which the tax incidence fell disproportionately on the rich but with some small amount of tax paid by those below the poverty line and with all the tax revenue transferred to the poor. Now consider expanding the scheme so that it also reaches people just barely above the poverty line and suppose that the cost of reaching them was less than that of reaching the poor. How much cheaper should it be to reach the almost poor before they are brought into the scheme? A poverty-reduction objective would never recommend expanding the program to the almost poor.

Of course, all these examples are artificial because they depend on comparing gains between those just below the poverty line and those just above it. If the poverty line were higher enough in any of these examples, the ranking of policies under a poverty-reduction objective could be reversed to agree with the ranking under a social welfare function. This suggests that policy analysis with a poverty-reduction objective and a range of poverty lines is less likely to produce anomalous results than one with a single poverty line—and every range needs an upper bound.

The Criteria for Setting the Range of Poverty Lines for the World Bank

That poverty measures are not grounded in mainstream economics and that poverty-reduction objectives are not widely accepted for policy analysis are not compelling arguments against the judicious use of poverty-reduction objectives. In many ways, the global poverty measures that are widely reported by the World Bank [headcount poverty rate, poverty gap, and squared poverty gap, based principally on the work of Chen, Datt, and Ravallion (1994) and Chen and Ravallion (2001)] in such publications as World Development Indicators and the World Development Report are similar to the human development index (HDI), widely used by the United Nations Development Programme, or measures of "unmet basic needs," widely used in Latin America. While none of these measures is grounded in mainstream welfare economics,

The World Bank Research Observer, vol. 21, no. 1 (Spring 2006)

they have an important and legitimate twofold purpose: public policy advocacy and organizational coherence around a clear mission and mandate.

The World Bank's objective should be global and national poverty reduction, and making those objectives operational requires a specification of the range of poverty lines (and the weighting functions that define particular poverty measures). One range of global poverty lines would divide the world's population into three categories: those below the lower bound poverty line who are indisputably poor, those who are above the upper bound poverty line who are indisputably not poor, and those in between who are poor by some standards but not by others. The key question is: For the World Bank's use of a poverty-reduction objective in its global policy advocacy and its organizational mission and mandate, what are the best lower and upper bounds on poverty lines?

There is widespread agreement that the $1 a day standard is an acceptable lower bound. In setting poverty lines, there was a fear that using a high poverty line would lead to accusations that the World Bank was "overstating" poverty in order to expand its mandate or funding, thus detracting from effective advocacy. The decision was made to choose a lower bound that was so low that no one could reasonably dispute that anyone living below this line was poor. But the same reasons that make $1 a day a good lower bound—that it is ultrapenurious—make it a bad choice as an upper bound. By the $1 a day standard only 6.6 percent of Sri Lankans, 11.3 percent of Bolivians, 12.3 percent of Ivorians, and 15.2 percent of Indonesians are poor. No one is really comfortable saying that a standard this low is the only reasonable global standard for poverty. After all, the $1 a day standard is, by construction, well below nearly all national poverty lines.

Since there is agreement that measuring global poverty requires a range of poverty lines and that $1 a day is a reasonable lower bound, the only remaining problem is to set an upper bound. Setting an upper bound is fundamentally about deciding who is not poor.[3] The problem of deciding who is not poor goes deep. If poverty is an unacceptable deprivation in material well-being, this implies that well-being of the nonpoor is acceptable. Moreover, if poverty reduction is an organization's objective, then income gains above the upper bound count for nothing. Strikingly, the problem of setting an upper bound has received almost no attention (an important exception, discussed below, is Atkinson and Bourguignon 2000).

What are the criteria that the World Bank should use in producing a GPL^{UB}?

- For an international organization, global poverty lines should be "globally inclusive" (Atkinson and Bourguignon 2000) or, as Bhalla (2002) puts it (with a little help from his friend), in setting the poverty line we should "imagine there's no country." Equivalent levels of well-being should count equally no matter where a person lives.
- The method for computing the upper bound should be consistent with the method for computing the lower bound.

- Since poverty reduction is used for measuring progress toward organizational objectives, the upper bound should be consistent with the well-grounded analytics and a reasonable conception of the activities encompassed by poverty reduction as an objective so that it can comfortably be said that income gains above the upper bound really count for zero in an organization's normative objectives.
- Since poverty reduction is used for policy advocacy, the upper bound should truly be the point at which people are not poor, and deprivation at that level of income should truly be acceptable.

The following section shows that a standard such as $10 a day (or higher) is a defensible upper bound, whereas treating $2 a day as an upper bound is indefensible.

A Modest Proposal for Bound Global Poverty Lines and What They Might Mean

This section first describes how the lower bound poverty line was set and argues that the upper bound should be set symmetrically. It examines the empirical implications of the resulting upper bound poverty line—that roughly 2–3 billion more people are included in global poverty, and then shows that these implications for global poverty are not unreasonable.

Methodological Consistency for the Lower and Upper Bounds

A poverty line can be defined, using the usual expenditure function $e(p, U)$, as the minimal expenditures necessary to achieve a given level of utility, with characteristics X of household H and the prices the household faces:

$$\text{Poverty line}^H = e(\text{prices}^H, X^H, U^{\text{Poverty}})$$

The expenditure function approach emphasizes that the level of well-being below which someone is considered poor, U^{Poverty}, is a social (and political) issue, not a technical one. Once U^{Poverty} is chosen, there are many technical aspects to constructing a poverty line [Ravallion (1993) is a classic reference]. Making appropriate comparisons requires taking into account household characteristics (see, for example, Deaton 1998a, 1998b) and variations in prices across space and time (Bidani and Ravallion 1993; Suryahadi, Sumarto, and Pritchett 2003) and across reference groups (Pradhan and others 2003). But the choice of U^{Poverty} itself, the threshold level of what is an "unacceptable" level of well-being, is unavoidably entirely a social convention.

The $1 a day standard was first adopted for *World Development Report 1990: Poverty* (World Bank 1990). Ravallion, Datt, and van de Walle's (1991) analysis of the national poverty lines of 36 poor countries found that while poverty lines tended to increase with country mean income, there seemed to be a lower bound below which poverty lines did not go even as countries got poorer. The choice was made to adopt the social convention that the global poverty line lower bound should be based on the poverty lines of the 10 poorest countries. That was the method: choose a GPL^{LB} near the national poverty lines of the poorest countries.

There is widespread belief that the $1 a day standard is determined by the cost of achieving a nutritionally adequate diet or of meeting basic physical needs and hence is grounded in biological facts and so is not merely a social convention. This is a myth, and while its serves the cultural function that myths often play admirably, it is factually false on two levels.

First, nutritional requirements never uniquely determine the food poverty line. Any calorie-based food poverty line can be expressed as the product of the number of calories and the cost per calorie, where the cost per calorie is determined by choosing a food basket. As people's income increases, the composition of their food basket changes in many ways: they eat more attractive staples (rice or wheat over cassava); they eat more fruits, vegetables, eggs, dairy, and meat; and they tend to eat more processed food (noodles). Nearly all these changes imply that the cost per calorie of people's actual consumption basket increases with income. The "nutritional requirements" method that is often applied by World Bank analysts uses the actual consumption basket of a "reference group" (usually households from a range of the income distribution). Other approaches use other methods of setting the consumption basket. But any method of setting the food basket (which determines the cost per calorie, which determines the food poverty line, and which determines the poverty line) is completely a social convention, not a biological fact.[4]

Second, the $1 a day global poverty line is not the average of all poverty lines set by the nutritional requirements approach. What pins down $1 a day as the GPL^{LB} is not a nutritional requirements approach, but rather a social convention by which the World Bank chose to adopt only the poverty lines of the poorest countries in setting the lower bound. Countries with higher average incomes that used exactly the same nutritional requirements approach would produce national poverty lines higher than the $1 a day line.

Myths aside, as a social convention for setting a lower bound of who is indisputably poor, using the standards of the poorest countries is very persuasive. So persuasive that this article proposes that the upper bound should be set in the same way: an upper bound of who is indisputably not poor using the standards of the richest countries is equally persuasive.

This is a particularly appropriate social convention for the World Bank, which is controlled by its shareholders quite directly. The proposed method simply adopts the notion that the rich country shareholders of the World Bank mean the same thing by *poverty* no matter the color of people's skin or the country of their birth. The counterargument—that unacceptable deprivation in well-being at a global level is lower than the standard that rich countries apply to their own citizens—would violate the goal of a globally inclusive standard for poverty. When the relevant group is the local community or a region or a country, it is legitimate to adopt a socially relevant standard or a poverty line that is limited to a geographically delineated reference group. But for global poverty, the upper bound should be global.

Current practice in the World Bank is to report global poverty measures for only two poverty lines, the $1 a day and the $2 a day standards. As this makes the $2 a day standard the highest poverty line for which poverty figures are ever reported, it inevitably leads to the interpretation, however unintended, that the $2 a day standard is the GPL^{UB}.[5] But there is absolutely no methodological foundation for the $2 a day standard as an upper bound. Whereas it may be roughly the poverty line of some middle-income countries, this would justify it only as one of many possible intermediate poverty lines or as an alternative lower bound but not as an upper bound.

Implementing a High Upper Bound: How Many People are "Not Poor"?

There are a variety of ways of implementing a GPL^{UB}, based on rich country standards. The method best suited for the organizational realities of the World Bank might be to have each World Bank shareholder declare its standard for a global poverty line, with the proviso that the standard for global poverty can be no lower (but could be higher) than the poverty line (or its equivalent) that the country uses for its own citizens. As with many other decisions made by the World Bank, the global poverty line could be a shareholder-weighted average of member country-proposed poverty lines. A companion paper (Pritchett 2003) shows that this (and many other plausible methods) produces a GPL^{UB} that is at least $10 a day (often much higher). For purposes of illustrating the implications of a higher upper bound standard, the $10 a day standard will be used here, in part because, at exactly 10 times the lower bound, it has nice "focal point" value.

The obvious implication of raising the global poverty line is that fewer people are not poor. Table 1 reports the two different estimates of the population falling into four categories: *destitute* (below $1 a day), *extreme poor* (below $2 a day), *global poor* (below $10 a day), and *not poor* (above the GPL^{UB}).

One estimate (labeled "author's calculation") uses data on real GDP per capita in purchasing power terms to establish the mean income and the assumption of log-normality along with distributional data to estimate the distribution of income. A uniform scaling factor is applied across all countries to reproduce exactly the estimate of poverty at the $2 a day standard reported in *World Development Indicators*

Table 1. Estimates of Headcount Poverty Rates and Number of Poor People Using Various Global Poverty Lines

International standards for degrees of poverty	Income or consumption expenditure per capita ($ in 1985 prices and P$ in 2000 prices)		Share of world population below this poverty line (headcount poverty, percent)			Number of poor people[a]	
	Per day	Per year	World Bank (2003)	POVCAL[b]	Author's calculation (described in text)		
Destitute	$1/P$1.50	$365/P$547	19.6	17.9	20.5	World Bank (2003)	1.21
						POVCAL	1.1
						Author's calculation	1.3
Extreme poverty	$2/P$3.00	$730/P$1,095	46.8	49.9	46.8 (by assumption)	World Bank (2003)	1.68
						POVCAL	2.0
						Author's calculation	1.6
Global poverty	$10/P$15.00	$3,650/P$5,475		81.5	87.9	World Bank (2003)	0
						POVCAL	2.0
						Author's calculation	2.5
Not poor	Above any upper bound poverty line			18.5	12.1	World Bank (2003)	3.3
						POVCAL	1.1
						Author's calculation	0.75

Source: Author's analysis as described in text.

a. Calculated by applying headcount rates to a population of 6.2 billion.

b. POVCAL does not have data for high-income countries, so headcount poverty rates of zero at $2 a day and 10 percent at $10 a day are assumed for these countries.

2003 (World Bank 2003).[6] By this higher standard, 88 percent of the world's population is among the global poor or, put differently, only 12 percent of the world's population is definitively not poor. At the $2 a day standard, 53 percent of the world's population is reported to be not poor—a difference of 2.5 billion people. A second calculation, using the POVCAL poverty estimation tool now available on the World Bank's website (http://www.worldbank.org/lsms/tools/povcal), produces estimates of headcount poverty of 17.9 percent at $1 a day, 49.9 percent at $2 a day, and 81.5 percent at $10 a day. Again, 2 billion people are in global poverty but not in extreme poverty.

The estimates are somewhat crude, but refinements will not overturn the basic point:[7] a poverty-reduction objective with a low poverty line such as $2 a day as an upper bound implies that, on a completely arbitrary basis, billions of people count for nothing in the World Bank's poverty-reduction objectives, who would count using a higher GPLUB that is consistent with rich country standards.

Table 2 presents estimates of headcount poverty rates for several countries to make the implications of the various poverty lines as stark as possible. Using $2 a day as an upper bound implies that income gains to people in the 17th percentile in Brazil or the 18th percentile in Turkey do not contribute to global poverty reduction. Even in poor countries like Côte d'Ivoire or Egypt, the $2 a day standard would imply that gains to people near the median income have zero value in reducing global poverty. In contrast, at the proposed higher poverty line, nearly everyone in poor countries is "globally poor" and only people in roughly the top quintile in middle-income countries like Brazil, Mexico, and Turkey are "not poor."[8]

Tables 1 and 2 report only the headcount poverty rate. One argument against high poverty lines is that by making nearly everyone globally poor, they render the

Table 2. Estimates of Headcount Poverty Rates for Global Poverty for Selected Countries

| Country | Year | World Bank (2001) estimates | | $10 a day (P$15) | |
		$1 a day (P$1.50)	$2 a day (P$3.00)	Author's calculation[a]	POVCAL
United States	2001	0	0.07	12.1	—
Brazil	1997	5.1	17.4	66.7	78.5
Turkey	1994	2.4	18.0	79.1	85.1
Mexico	1995	17.9	42.5	92.2	86.2
Côte d'Ivoire	1995	12.3	49.6	98.9	98.4
Egypt	1995	13.1	52.6	99.7	98.5
India	1997	44.2	86.2	99.9	99.5

Source: World Bank (2001) (table 4) and author's analysis as described in the text.

[a]Estimates are based on the assumption of log-normality (using Gini coefficients to estimate variance of the log normal). In each case, GDP per capita in purchasing power parity terms is scaled to match reported $2 a day estimates from the World Bank (2001) and so the $2 and $10 a day estimates are comparable.

headcount measure—which, it is argued, is the only poverty measure most people can understand—virtually useless. But this is a weak argument, as everyone acknowledges that the headcount cannot be taken seriously as a policy objective at *any* poverty line. Perhaps using a reasonable GPL[UB] would help to highlight the importance of using weights in constructing poverty measures rather than relying on the headcount.

Estimates of Global Poverty with a High Upper Bound are Reasonable

Several arguments can be made for why the claim that most very poor countries are "globally poor" is believable.

First, Dani Rodrik (2005) calculated the income in purchasing power parity terms of the "rich" (defined as the top 10 percent) in a poor country (defined as the bottom 10 percent of countries) and the "poor" (defined as the bottom 10 percent) in a rich country. By this calculation, the income of a "rich" individual in a "poor" country is P\$2,800 (P\$7 a day), whereas the income of a "poor" individual in a "rich" country is nearly three times as high at P\$8,640 (P\$23 a day). It is not surprising, therefore, that if the poverty line were set so that the bottom 10 percent of the richest country population is taken as 'globally poor' that even someone well above the 90th percentile in the poorest 10 percent of countries would be globally poor. Figure 1, adapted from *World Development Report 2006: Equity and Development* (World Bank 2006), shows the 90th/10th percentile ratios for selected countries. Although based on different data than the calculations above, the basic point comes through clearly. Even after adjusting for purchasing power, the 10th percentile of the U.S. income distribution is well above the 90th percentile of nearly all poor countries.

There is still some resistance to the view that "the rich" in poor countries are globally poor. One reason is the confusion of "the rich" in the economist's sense of being in the upper percentiles of the income distribution—top 20 percent, 10 percent, or 5 percent—with "the rich" in the popular sense of *Forbes* magazine or the newspaper society pages or F. Scott Fitzgerald's "Let me tell you about the very rich. They are different from you and me." The typical wages paid to experienced servants or drivers for an expatriate family or a super rich family in New Delhi place these individuals well above the 95th percentile for urban households (and hence easily into the 99th percentile nationwide). These servants of the super rich in the capital are the "income distribution rich" in India. Thus, it is a gross misconception to associate "the rich" in India exclusively with the super rich Tatas or Oberois or Ambanis or Birlas or Mittals (one of whom was the world's third richest person in a recent list), who make up just a small fraction of the top percentile of the income distribution.

This misconception is perpetuated by reference to the percentiles of the income distribution without emphasizing that the absolute gap that separates the "average"

Figure 1. Between Country Comparison of Income or Consumption Expenditure Box–Whisker Plots for the 10th and 90th Percentiles, Mean and Median

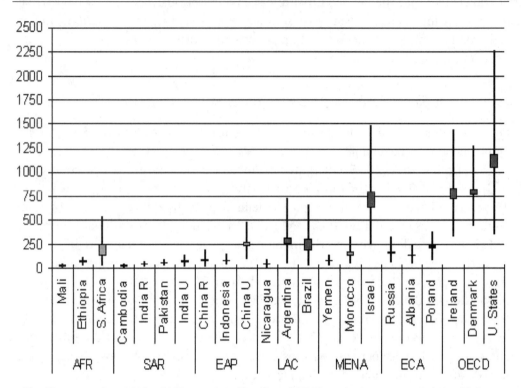

Note: Years range from 1996 to 2002 as measured by adjusted (1993 purchasing power parity) monthly income or consumption.

Source: World Bank 2006, figure 3.6.

individual from the rich (in the 95th or 99th percentile) is small compared with the gap between the rich and the super rich. For instance, in India the difference in annual per capita income in 1999/2000 between the median per capita income and the 95th percentile was around P$1,750. Using tax data to estimate the gap between the 99th percentile and the 99.5th percentile, Banerjee and Piketty (2005) find that it was four times as large—almost P$7,000—as the gap between the "typical" person and the "income distribution rich" at the 95th percentile. The Indian super rich at the 99.99th percentile with annual incomes of about P$160,000 per person are very rich indeed—and they have incomes astronomically higher than even those in the 95th percentile.

A more serious argument against the view that the "the rich" in poor countries are globally poor is that even if one accepts that the purchasing power conversions are correct on average for comparing national aggregates, comparing the incomes of various parts of the income distribution is not legitimate. People frequently claim that the rich in poor countries live much better on the same income than people in rich countries because labor is so much cheaper in poor countries. But the question is not whether labor and prices are much cheaper in poor countries—of course they are—and that is why all income comparisons are adjusted using purchasing power currency conversions rather than official exchanges rates. The question is whether the well-being of the richer households in poor countries is substantially under-stated relative to that of the poor with equivalent purchasing power incomes in rich countries.

One way of checking for systematic bias is to examine whether some nonmone-tary indicator of well-being—for example, child mortality, malnutrition, child edu-cation, or a proxy such as share of income spent on food—varies systematically between the rich in poor countries and the poor in rich countries. Consider the case of child mortality among the richest 20 percent of the population (as measured by an asset index; Gwatkin and others 2001; Filmer and Pritchett 2001) for 45 poor countries ordered by their average purchasing power-adjusted gross domestic policy (GDP) per capita (figure 2). For all countries with average GDP per capita below the $2 a day, threshold child mortality among the richest 20 percent of households is more than 10 times the average among the poorest in Organisation for Economic Co-operation and Development (OECD) countries. For all countries with GDP per capita of less than $10 a day, child mortality is still much higher among the richest 20 percent of the population and is more than three times the OECD average.

Thus, comparing infant mortality rates suggests that the highest quintile in even middle-income countries is worse off than the poorest quintile in the OECD. The com-panion paper (Pritchett 2003) performs the same exercise for malnutrition, school-ing attainment, and the food share, with similar results. Thus, there is no reason to believe that purchasing power-adjusted indicators of income systematically over-state the well-being of the rich in poor countries compared with the poor in rich countries—if anything, the opposite is true.

A related point is the concern that an exclusive focus on the income or expendi-ture dimension of poverty is inconsistent with other goals, such as the Millenium Development Goals for education or health or nutrition. But as the companion paper (Pritchett 2003) shows at some length, as $2 a day households have not put all their children in school, infant mortality is not low, and malnutrition still exists. If the poverty line were defined as the level of income at which people typically achieve acceptable levels of the Millennium Development Goal indicators (such as universal primary school completion), it would be set at about $10 a day.

Another common reaction to the proposed upper bound is that the $1 a day and $10 a day poverty lines are just too far apart. But statistics provides intuition only about how large ranges or confidence intervals should be in units scaled by standard deviations not in absolute terms. Since the lower and upper bound poverty lines are based on country poverty lines that are related to country incomes, the poverty lines

Figure 2. Child Mortality among the Richest 20 Percent of Households

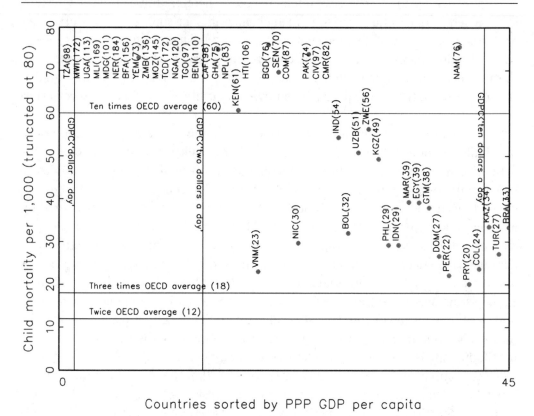

Countries sorted by PPP GDP per capita

Source: Author's calculations based on Filmer and Pritchett (2001).

are far apart because the income gaps across countries are so large. One standard deviation below mean (natural log) GDP per capita (in P$985) is about $3 a day, whereas one standard deviation above the mean is $28.80 a day—a ratio of 9.35. So, if the poor were defined as those more than one standard deviation below the international mean (log) income and the not poor as those more than one standard deviation above that mean, with the remainder being poor by some standards and not by others, then if GDP per capita were log normally distributed, the lower and upper bounds would be expected to be at about a ratio of 10:1, with 16 percent poor, 16 percent not poor, and 68 percent poor or not poor depending on the standard.

A slightly different line of argument is that poor people in rich countries are not "really" poor. At $2 a day, essentially no one in the United States is poor: not inner city African–Americans living in crime-infested neighborhoods, not Native Americans on rural reservations where unemployment tops 50 percent, not immigrants in the informal economy working two and three jobs, or not people living in declining rural areas. No one is saying that these people are as poor as the poor in Africa or rural India or that they deserve equal concern (again, any reasonable poverty measure is intensity weighted). But asserting that the $2 a day standard should apply globally for poverty is to assert that the living standard of everyone in the United States is globally acceptable. Again, poverty as a social construct can be debated, but I personally do not have a normative objective function in which no American is poor.

Atkinson and Bourguignon (2000) address the problem that the low poverty lines of $1 a day and $2 a day do not adequately capture world poverty. They stress that a standard for global poverty should be inclusive because "national boundaries have no intrinsic status." They also propose the use of very high poverty lines. The principal difference is that they regard the higher poverty lines as based on "relative" poverty. Their empirical measure assumes a person is poor if that person has an income either below the absolute poverty line of $1 a day or below 40 percent of the mean GDP per capita of the country of residence. The second measure implies some very high poverty lines: in 2003, it would be $41 a day in the United States.

The principal objection to this approach is that it does not meet the authors' own criterion of being "world inclusive" because poverty depends on where a person lives. By their proposed poverty standards, someone living at the mean income in India (and so above $1 a day) is not among the global poor, but someone living at 35 percent of mean GDP per capita in France is among the global poor—despite the fact that the income of the person in France (as always, adjusted for purchasing power) is four times higher. Moreover, every nonmonetary indicator of well-being (health, nutrition, and schooling) also suggests that the Indian household at the 50th percentile is much worse off than the French household at 40 percent of GDP per capita. There certainly seems to be little evidence that people at the 40th percentile in OECD countries care so much about their relative deprivation that they would accept a much lower absolute standard of living but higher relative rank by moving to a much poorer country where they would find themselves at, say, the 50th percentile. The goal of a "world inclusive" standard for poverty would suggest a common set of poverty lines.

What a Higher Upper Bound Poverty Line Would Mean for the World Bank

Poverty reduction is rightly the World Bank's mission and mandate: its dream should be a world free of poverty. But that vision is seriously compromised if the dream ends abruptly and arbitrarily at $2 a day. A low upper bound for the global poverty line (such as $2 a day) creates needless inconsistency between a poverty-reduction measure and the organization's mission and mandate in at least four ways: arbitrary exclusion of concern for people with low levels of well-being, inconsistency with national poverty lines, inconsistency with a broad development agenda for global equity, and inconsistency with a goal of broad-based growth.

Less Arbitrary and More Robust

The $2 a day standard is arbitrarily an upper bound poverty line and so cannot be taken as precise. But because a low upper bound poverty line such as the $2 a day standard cuts through a very thick section of the world income distribution, minor imprecision has big implications. If the standard were only $0.45 a day higher (a tiny amount in a rich country), 500 million people change from not poor to poor. At just 10 percent higher, some 220 million people—the population of a country, the size of Indonesia, or twice that of Bangladesh—would be included in the objective of poverty reduction. In contrast, the $10 a day upper bound cuts across a thinner part of the income distribution. Adding $0.45 per day to the poverty line would add just 36 million people to those considered to be poor, not 500 million.[9]

National Poverty Lines within the Global Range

In its engagement in national policy and lending the World Bank should use national poverty lines that are relevant to the social and economic realities of the country. With a high upper bound global poverty rate, the World Bank can comfortably engage in country-based policy dialogue around any sensibly set national poverty line that lies between its lower and upper global bounds. A low global upper bound such as $2 a day puts many national poverty lines above that upper bound, creating a potential contradiction in the poverty agenda.

One of the lines of criticism of the World Bank by the Meltzer Commission report (IFIAC 2000) and others is crudely summarized—if poverty is your objective, get out of most countries because they have very few poor people. Many others have used the World Bank's consistent reporting of global poverty only at low poverty lines to argue that the World Bank should get out of International Bank for Reconstruction and Development (IBRD) lending and into grants exclusively because it should not be providing assistance only in places where "global poverty" is very low. Adopting a reasonable upper bound poverty line (and using a more broadly conceived notion of poverty, along the lines of World Bank 2001) dissipates the force of these arguments in a consistent and reasonable way.[10]

A Development Agenda for Nations

A low upper bound makes it difficult to engage in the broad range of issues that are crucial to development. When poverty reduction is the objective, any public policy action—reducing corruption, improving service delivery, reforming the financial sector, improving port infrastructure, raising school quality, and improving health system financing—has to be considered from the perspective of how it benefits the poor. There is no justification for a monopoly on defining what "the poor" means in this context. And a focus on poverty reduction is itself no reason to exclude the 2–3 billion people who are below a reasonable GPL^{UB}.

Consider two quick examples, using poverty rates in Côte d'Ivoire as an illustration. In 1995, headcount poverty was 12.3 percent at $1 a day, 49.6 percent at $2 a day, and 98 percent at $10 a day (see table 2). Thus, by the descriptions of poverty proposed in table 1, very few people were destitute, about half were extremely poor, and nearly everyone was globally poor. With an upper bound of $2 a day, half the population of Côte d'Ivoire was not poor. What are the development issues that should be on the table in Côte d'Ivoire, and how is this list affected by poverty lines? Suppose the World Bank were to support an action that would reduce corruption or improve schooling or transport and would benefit everyone in Côte d'Ivoire by an equal absolute amount. By the goal of reducing global poverty with a high upper bound, this is a big gain. But with a $2 a day standard, this project risks being judged a failure because half of the benefits went to the not poor.

In a second example, suppose that by supporting some combination of policy and institutional reforms, the World Bank were able to contribute to the acceleration of economic growth by 5 percentage points in Côte d'Ivoire, sustained over 10 years. Suppose that this growth were distributionally neutral, with everyone's incomes increasing by the same proportional amount. A big development success, right? Wrong. Using the $1 a day standard, the "poor" would receive only about 3.5 percent of the total gains, and so if the poverty-reduction objective is taken literally then $96.50 of every $100 in gains from these reforms had zero value because it went to the not poor.[11] So with low poverty lines, a poverty-reduction objective becomes a rhetorical trap: reform that ignites broad-based growth in a very poor country—where among the richest 20 percent of the population the infant mortality rate was 63.3, where one child in three did not finish grade five, where malnutrition affected one in nine children—is a failure because almost $97 of every $100 does not reach the "poor." Moving to a $2 a day standard mitigates this problem somewhat, but it remains severe. A high poverty line, however, makes it clear that accelerated broad-based growth in Côte d'Ivoire is a huge gain for poverty reduction.

It is increasingly understood that poverty reduction requires a broad array of activities that include both systemic changes and targeted activities. While microfinance projects might reach the poorest of the poor, a well functioning financial system also contributes to development. While targeted transfers help the poorest children attend school, overall improvements in learning achievement are also needed for development. While the poorest people need empowerment to protect them from abuse by the police and the legal apparatus, countries also need a police and legal apparatus that works for all. While the poorest people in rural areas need all-weather connecting roads, development requires national highways as well. A development institution like the IBRD, for instance, should be engaged in global poverty reduction in a way that balances actions aimed at reaching the poorest of the poor with actions aimed at broad-based development of poorer countries. The exclusive use of low global poverty lines is a needlessly narrow foundation for development activities that would reduce global poverty at a reasonable standard for who is poor and who is not poor.

A Global Policy Agenda

Poverty is high on the world's agenda today, with debates about how to promote "pro-poor" growth and about whether globalization has been favorable to the poor. But the quantitative answers to these questions hinge on how *poverty* is defined. For instance, in India there is some evidence that the rapid economic growth of the 1990s, which many people associate with increased globalization of the Indian economy, reduced poverty as measured by the national poverty line less than expected (for example, Deaton and Kozel 2005). Does this mean that globalization was not pro-poor? Of course not. Broad-based growth in India is enormously pro-"global"-poor, a point that consistent use of a high GPL^{UB} alongside the low national poverty line would make abundantly clear.

That is not to say that efforts to make growth more pro-poor by national standards are not important in India and elsewhere—they are. But the high growth rates in India, China, and Vietnam during a period of increased market orientation have been accompanied by what is likely the most rapid reduction in global poverty in the history of humankind (Besley and Burgess 2003). The question of whether such broad phenomena as globalization have been good for the global poor should not be limited to whether they have been good for the destitute (a separate and also interesting question) or whether they have been relatively good for those below national poverty lines.

A high GPL^{UB} is useful in discussions of inequality because it puts differences across individuals within countries and across countries on the same footing. Nearly all measures of inequality are made and reported country by country. Also, national poverty lines often depend on national income and so emphasize comparisons only within countries. But far and away, the greatest component of inequality is the differences across countries (Bourguignon and Morrison 2002). Poverty has been reduced primarily through economic growth that has enabled mean incomes in poor countries to gain on incomes in rich countries (Kraay 2004).

Although it may serve some interests to take international inequality off the table, there is no reason to focus exclusively on national inequalities. Nor is there any reason not to make poverty comparisons based on the notion that all people can attain the standards of living now enjoyed in OECD countries. As *World Development Report*

2006: Equity and Development (World Bank 2006) stresses, there is no reason why a typical Indian citizen should be compared only with other Indians. There is no reason why equity as fundamental fairness should not be compared on a global basis.

Conclusion

This article has reviewed the major lacuna in the World Bank's measurement of global income or consumption expenditure poverty, which is one important element of its broader objective of multidimensional poverty reduction: how to set the GPL^{UB}. Everyone agrees that there is no uniquely adequate poverty line, but rather that a range of poverty lines should be considered. There is little disagreement that the widely adopted $1 a day standard is a very conservative, and hence reasonable, lower bound. But whereas the notion that people living on less than a $1 a day are poor is widely accepted, the notion that people living on $1.01 a day are not poor is not. However, there is no agreement on what would constitute a reasonable upper bound—and very little discussion. A GPL^{UB} should be set so that it is agreed that people above that line are not poor. If poverty reduction is the objective, then the income gains to those at the upper bound should really merit more than zero concern.

The World Bank's practice of reporting regional and aggregate global poverty measures only at two alternative lower bounds—$1 and $2 a day—creates the temptation to interpret the higher of the alternative lower bounds as the upper bound. There is no methodological, analytical, organizational, or normative basis for treating $2 a day as an upper bound, and doing so creates serious problems.

There is a very simple and obvious solution: adopting a methodologically consistent procedure for setting the lower and upper bound poverty lines. Just as the national poverty lines of the poorest countries were adopted as the lower bound, the national poverty lines of the rich countries can be used to establish an upper bound. The goal would be to estimate those who are poor by various standards—the destitute (below a lower bound), the not poor (above an upper bound), and a broad range of people who are poor by some standards but not by others.

The implications of adopting a high GPL^{UB} are not trivial. Between 2 and 3 billion people considered not poor at a low upper bound are considered globally poor by this higher standard. And while the headcount measure is analytically problematic as a normative objective with any poverty line, with a high poverty line the issue of the appropriate weights in the poverty measure becomes even more important. These new multiple measures of poverty with different intensity weights should be added to the reporting of poverty measures at the lower bound of the $1 a day standard (perhaps relabeled 'destitution') and the intermediate bound of $2 a day (perhaps relabeled "extreme poverty").

The danger with rhetoric is that people might take it seriously. If the World Bank says that "everything we do should be judged in terms of poverty reduction" and then reports exclusively on measures of global poverty at low poverty lines, this creates an unnecessary tension. There is no empirical evidence or compelling analytical rationale that exclusively applying low poverty lines is good for the poor in any case. A poverty discourse based globally on three standards: destitution, extreme poverty, and global poverty, combined with a national policy discourse based on national poverty lines, arguably provides the most solid basis for the World Bank's organizational mission and policy advocacy. Everything the World Bank does should be about poverty—with the right definitions of poverty.

Notes

Lant Pritchett is lead socio-economist in the Social Development Unit of the South Asia Region at the World Bank; his e-mail address is lpritchett@worldbank.org. The author thanks many people for comments or conversations that have been helpful to the writing of this review—all without the implication that they agree with any of the arguments—Angus Deaton, Deon Filmer, Aart Kraay, Jeffrey Hammer, Rinku Murgai, John Page, Martin Ravallion, Geeta Sethi, Michael Walton, Michael Woolcock, and Roberto Zagha. The editor and the editorial board of the *World Bank Research Observer* have also dragged many improvements from a reluctant author.

1. Inflation wrecks havoc with the use of simple focal point numbers like $1 a day or $2 a day. Since the $1 a day standard was created based on 1985 purchasing power parity-adjusted current units (normalized to U.S. prices), there has been roughly 50 percent inflation in those prices in the 15 years to 2000. This means that the $1 a day standard is really about $1.50 a day in 2000 prices and the $2 a day standard is about $3 a day. To reduce confusion, poverty lines based on 1985 prices are shown simply as $1 a day or $10 a day, whereas those based on 2000 prices use the notation P$ for purchasing power-adjusted current units normalized to U.S. prices. Thus $1 a day and P$1.50 a day or $10 a day and P$15 a day refer to the same standard, with the P$ notation simply indicating adjustment for inflation in the base currency.

2. As World Bank (2001) emphasizes, poverty is a complex, multidimensional phenomenon, which makes any unmodified use of the word *poverty* problematic. The only dimension of poverty considered here is a single monetized measure of well-being, which in empirical practice is a measure either of income or of consumption expenditures. This is not to assert that this measure captures the most important dimension of poverty. The broad definition of poverty in World Bank (2001) supports many different kinds of poverty measures: "human capability poverty" as a deprivation in human capabilities (Sen 1999), "empowerment poverty" as unacceptable deprivation in control over important dimensions of one's life, "human investment poverty" as an unacceptable deprivation of children's ability to attain the skills they need to be productive adults in a modern society, and even Adam Smith's notion of "shame poverty" or an unacceptable deprivation in the ability "to walk in public without shame." For simplicity, the word *poverty* is used in this article without any modifier to mean income or consumption expenditure poverty.

3. The implications of setting the bound too low and of saying that someone is not poor when they are poor have not been fully explored. There is an analogy with the statistics of type I and type II errors. Conventions about the levels of type I error (such as the 1 percent, 5 percent, and 10 percent levels of statistical significance) are purposely conservative, even when these lead to low power (a high probability of failing to reject a hypothesis that is false, or a type II error). But there is no compelling case for why a poverty line should be set conservatively enough to avoid "falsely" saying that someone is poor

when they are not. Thus, using two extreme lines has some appeal. One can be sure that someone below the lowest line is truly poor—but there is a good chance that someone just above that line is also poor. By the same token, one can be reasonably sure that someone above the GPL^{UB} is not poor, but at some risk that even some who are below the line are also not poor.

4. Once it is shown that the food poverty line is determined by the choice of the quality of foods in the basket and that choice is a social convention about the level of well-being that defines poverty, then it is no longer clear why food has pride of place. That is, if the quality of food in the food basket is determined by a "conversation" about the appropriate level of well-being at which it is appropriate to say that people are poor in a given social situation, then why not also include a convention about housing or clothing or transport or health care? No good reason, really. Moreover, a "subjective" approach to setting a poverty line—simply asking people what they think a poverty line should be—is a common approach and has equal claim to legitimacy as the nutritionally based approaches since both are determined by social convention. One could combine approaches and use subjective responses to pin down a level and expenditure functions to maintain comparability.

5. Even those who argue that the World Bank has mismeasured progress on poverty adopt by default the $2 a day standard (see Sala-i-Martin 2002a; 2002b; *The Economist*, March 11, 2004; and the response by Ravallion 2004).

6. This is an examination of the implications of various poverty lines, not an independent estimate of poverty in the world.

7. These numbers are also consistent with (Sala-i-Martin 2002a, 2002b) distribution of income based on a crude "eyeball" estimate of almost 19 percent poverty at $2 a day and more than 70 percent for poverty at $10 a day. These estimates are mentioned with some caution as Ravallion (2004) points out that this means of computing poverty is riddled with methodological problems. However, while this method does produce estimates that are "too low" in absolute levels, over time his $1 a day estimates correspond almost exactly to the $2 a day estimates from official World Bank sources, and his $2 a day estimate corresponds to the 19.6 percent poverty estimate of World Bank (2003). In any case, only the difference in headcount poverty rates between the two poverty lines is relevant, not the absolute level at any given poverty line.

8. This clear alternative creates a very simple test of whether this article has simply created and attacked a straw man. The World Bank publishes annual reports that include a variety of poverty measures—such as the *World Development Indicators* and the *World Development Report*. With POVCAL, it is technically easy to compute poverty measures at a variety of poverty lines. If the $2 a day standard is not an upper bound, then at least one official publication should be willing to report measures of global poverty by country and for regional aggregates at the World Bank's real upper bound. If $2 a day is the World Bank's GPL^{UB}, then it should be defended as such. The intermediate position—"the highest poverty line we will ever officially publish poverty measures for is not our upper bound"—seems indefensible.

9. The exact figures depend on the assumption of log-normality of each country's income distribution, and so are illustrative only.

10. The assertion of a high upper bound is not a self-serving rationalization to maintain lending. It is a reassertion of the core mission and mandate of the World Bank for development. Moreover, it is the practice of using a lower bound as an upper bound that never had any rationale. In any case, nothing about setting the poverty line asserts that World Bank *lending* is the key value added. The World Bank offers a complex array of services and levels and types of engagement according to country circumstances. To argue that it is legitimate to be engaged with Turkey or Mexico, or Brazil or Egypt in the interests of global poverty is not to deny the possibility of substitutability between private and multilateral lending. The debates about World Bank value added and effectiveness are conceptually distinct from the question of whether, no matter how effective, the actions could contribute to the objectives.

11. In World Bank (2001), the 1995 consumption shares were 3.1 percent for the bottom 10 percent and 7.1 percent for the bottom 20 percent. If the poor are 12.3 percent of the population, they account for something like 3.5 percent of consumption.

References

Atkinson, A. B., and F. Bourguignon. 2000. "Poverty and Inclusion from a World Perspective." In H. De la Largentaye, P.-A.Muet, J.-F.Rischard, and J. E. Stiglitz, eds., *Governance, Equity, and Global Markets*. Paris: La Documentation Française.

Banerjee, Abhijt, and Thomas Piketty. 2005. "Top Indian Incomes, 1922–2000." *World Bank Economic Review* 19(1):1–20.

Besley, Timothy, and Robin Burgess. 2003. "Halving World Poverty." *Journal of Economic Perspectives* 17(3):3–22.

Bhalla, Surjit S. 2002. *Imagine There's No Country: Poverty, Inequality, and Growth in the Era of Globalization*. Washington, D.C.: Institute for International Economics.

Bidani, B., and M. Ravallion. 1993. "A Regional Poverty Profile for Indonesia." *Bulletin of Indonesian Economic Studies* 29(1):53–83.

Bourguignon, Francois, and C. Morrisson. 2002. "Inequality among World Citizens: 1820–1990." *American Economic Review* 94(4):730–52.

Chen, Shaohua, Guarav Datt, and Martin Ravallion. 1994. "Is Poverty Increasing or Decreasing in the Developing World?" *Review of Income and Wealth* 40:359–76.

Chen, Shaohua, and Martin Ravallion. 2001. "How did the World's Poor fare in the 1990s?" *Review of Income and Wealth* 47(3):283–300.

Deaton, Angus. 1998a. *The Analysis of Household Surveys: a Microeconometric Approach to Development Policy*. Baltimore, M.D: The Johns Hopkins Press.

———. 1998b. "Economies of Scale, Household Size, and the Demand for Food." *Journal of Political Economy* 106(5):897–930.

Deaton, Angus, and Valerie Kozel. 2005. "Data and Dogma: The Great Indian Poverty Debate." *World Bank Research Observer* 20(2):177–99.

Filmer, Deon, and Lant Pritchett. 2001. "Estimating Wealth Effects without Expenditure Data or Tears: An Application to Educational Enrollments in States of India." *Demography* 38(1):15–32.

Gwatkin, Davidson, Shea Rutstein, Kiersten Johnson, Rohini Pande, and Adam Wagstaff. 2000. "Socio Economic Differences in Health, Nutrition, and Population in Bangladesh (and comparable publications covering Benin, Bolivia, Brazil, Burkina Faso, Cameron, Central African Republic, Colombia, Comores, Cote d'Ivoire, Dominican Republic, Ghana, Guatemala, Haiti, India, Indonesia, Kenya, Kyrgyz Republic, Madagascar, Malawi, Mali, Morrocco, Mozambique, Namibia, Nepal, Nicaragua, Niger, Nigeria, Pakistan, Paraguay, Peru, Philippines, Senegal, Tanzania, Togo, Turkey, Uganda, Vietnam, Zambia, and Zimbabwe)." Washington, DC: The World Bank.

IFIAC (International Financial. Institution Advisory Commission). 2000. *"Report of the International Financial Institution. Advisory Commission."* Meltzer Commission Report, Washington, D.C.

Kraay, Aart. 2004. "When Is Growth Pro-Poor?: Cross-Country Evidence." Policy Research Working Paper Series 3225. World Bank, Washington, D.C.

Pradhan, Menno, Asep Suryahadi, Sudarno Sumarto, and Lant Pritchett. 2001. "Eating Like Which 'Joneses'? An Interactive Solution to the Choice of Poverty Line Reference Group." *Review of Income and Wealth* 47(4):473–87.

Pritchett, Lant. 2003. "Who Is Not Poor: Proposing a Higher International Standard for Poverty." Center for Global Development Working Paper 33. Washington, D.C.

Ravallion, Martin. 1993. "Poverty Comparisons: A Guide to Concepts and Methods." LSMS Working Paper 88. World Bank, Living Standards Measurement Study, Washington, D.C.

———. 2004. "Pessimistic on Poverty?" *The Economist*. April 10, p. 74.

Ravallion, Martin, Gaurav Datt, and Dominique van de Walle. 1991. "Quantifying Absolute Poverty in the Developing World." *Review of Income and Wealth* 37(4):345–61.

Rodrik, Dani. 2005. *"Lecture Notes on Economic Development: Theory, Evidence, Policy."* Harvard University, John F. Kennedy School of Government, Cambridge, Mass.

Sala-i-Martin, Xavier. 2002a. *The "Disturbing" Rise of Income Inequality.* NBER Working Paper 8933. National Bureau of Economic Research, Cambridge, MA.

———. 2002b. *The World Distribution of Income: Estimated from Individual Country Distributions.* NBER Working Paper 8933. National Bureau of Economic Research, Cambridge, MA.

Sen, Amartya. 1999. *Development as Freedom.* New York: Oxford University Press.

Suryahadi, Asep, Sudarno Sumarto, and Lant Pritchett. 2003. "The Evolution of Poverty during the Crisis in Indonesia." *Asian Economic Journal* 17(3):221–41.

World Bank. 1990. *World Development Report 1990: Poverty.* New York: Oxford University Press.

———. 2001. *World Development Report 2000/2001: Attacking Poverty.* New York: Oxford University Press.

———. 2003. *World Development Indicators 2003.* Washington, D.C.

———. 2006. *World Development Report 2006: Equity and Development.* New York and Washington, D.C: Oxford University Press and World Bank.

Reducing the Incidence of Low Birth Weight in Low-Income Countries Has Substantial Economic Benefits

Harold Alderman • Jere R. Behrman

Reducing the incidence of low birth weight not only lowers infant mortality rates but also has multiple benefits over the life cycle. This study estimates the economic benefits of reducing the incidence of low birth weight in low-income countries, both through lower mortality rates and medical costs and through increased learning and productivity. The estimated economic benefits, under plausible assumptions, are fairly substantial, at about $510 per infant moved from a low-birth-weight status. The estimated gains are primarily from increases in labor productivity (partially through more education) and secondarily from avoiding costs due to infant illness and death. Thus there may be many interventions to reduce the incidence of low birth weight that are warranted purely on the grounds of saving resources or increasing productivity.

Each year, some 11.7 million children in developing countries—16 percent of newborns—are born with low birth weight (weighing less than 2,500 g), most of them in low-income countries (UN SCN 2004). Many of these infants die young, contributing significantly to neonatal mortality. Many who survive infancy suffer cognitive and neurological impairment and are stunted as adults, all conditions that are associated with lower productivity in a range of educational, economic, and other activities. Low-birth-weight infants also may have increased risk of cardiovascular disease, diabetes, and hypertension later in life. For all these reasons, low birth weight appears to have serious economic costs.

Approach of the Current Analysis

This article synthesizes the relevant literature on low birth weight and, in a manner that is transparent and flexible to variations in core assumptions, provides the first

doi:10.1093/wbro/lkj001   Advance Access publication 12 January 2006   21:25–48 estimates of the total potential economic gains from reducing the incidence of low birth weight in low-income countries. Individual studies do not provide much insight into the potential overall gains from reducing the incidence of low birth weight, but this review combines the implications of several studies and some explicit assumptions to derive these estimates. The approach is general and can be applied to other health interventions that provide benefits through increased productivity and resource savings as well as through reduced illness and death.

This review differs from the Disease Control Priorities Project (Jamison and others 1993), which focuses on the relative cost-effectiveness of different health interventions but does not attempt to place benefits in a metric that allows comparison with other possible investments outside the health sector. The emphasis in this article is on estimating economic benefits in monetary terms. These benefits can, of course, be compared with the cost of obtaining them, as is done illustratively for a few promising programs—for example, an iron supplementation program in Nepal (Christian and others 2003).[1] However, even without experimental data on the cost of full-scale programs or in the absence of currently available low-cost technology, there is still value in knowing the potential benefits of new approaches to reducing low birth weight because such estimates can inform decisions about the value of efforts to spur research. For example, there are no fully effective vaccines for human immunodeficiency virus (HIV) or malaria, but estimates of the potential benefits are nevertheless useful for determining what resources should be devoted to research for vaccines. Similarly, although there are technologies for renewable solar energy, they are not yet low cost. Nevertheless, it is of value to know the breakeven point. The estimates provided here may likewise inform possible research on new techniques for reducing low birth weight.

To some extent this article parallels studies by Horton (1999) and Horton and Ross (2003). But although this study draws on the experience of the Disease Control Priorities Project and of Horton and colleagues, it differs in the subject for which benefits are calculated and in its emphasis on a method for varying core assumptions to accommodate diverse underlying conditions. In breaking down total benefits into components and their contribution to overall estimated gains, the study also points to where the gains to better information might be greatest.

This economic assessment of current information on the benefits of reducing the incidence of low birth weight in low-income countries is intended to clarify the economic case for the use of public resources for that purpose and to identify likely important research areas. It recognizes that not all returns are economic but that clarifying the economic returns will facilitate comparisons among alternatives. That should also shed light on how large the noneconomic returns must be to justify changing the priorities indicated by the economic returns.

The review first identifies the causes of low birth weight and its economic impacts. It then explores considerations involved in measuring the economic benefits of interventions to reduce the incidence of low birth weight. This is followed by a discussion of the empirical information on the benefits of reducing the incidence of low birth weight. Lastly, some simulations are presented of the overall benefits of reducing the incidence of low birth weight, and their sensitivity to alternative assumptions is considered.

Causes of Low Birth Weight and Its Economic Impacts

Prematurity and intrauterine growth retardation are the two main causes of low birth weight, with prematurity relatively more important in developed countries and intrauterine growth retardation in developing countries (Villar and Belizán 1982). Proximate determinants of prematurity include multiple births, stress, anxiety and other psychological factors, high maternal blood pressure, acute infections, and hard physical work (Kramer 1998). Proximate determinants of intrauterine growth retardation include abnormally small or blocked placenta and factors in the maternal environment that prevent normal circulation across the placenta and thus cause poor nutrient and oxygen supplies to the fetus. Maternal undernutrition, anemia, malaria, and acute and chronic infections (such as sexually transmitted infections and urinary tract infections) all contribute to this risk (Allen and Gillespie 2001; Verhoeff and others 2001).

The economic impacts of low birth weight may occur at various stages of the life cycle. It is useful to distinguish among three broad life-cycle stages.

Impacts in the Neonatal Period and Infancy

Low birth weight is associated with higher risk of illness and death, impaired immune function, and poorer cognitive development. There are important differences between intrauterine growth retardation and prematurity in the extent to which low-birth-weight babies tend to catch-up on growth in childhood. Although premature low-birth-weight babies tend to catch-up gradually with normal-birth-weight babies, babies suffering from intrauterine growth retardation tend to remain somewhat below the means in anthropometric distributions as children and adults.

Wherever possible this review attempts to focus more on intrauterine growth retardation than on prematurity. However, because prematurity is more prevalent in developed countries, where data tend to be better and analyses more extensive, this analysis occasionally has to infer from experiences of prematurity.

Low birth weight results in two main economic costs in infancy: those associated with early death and those associated with additional requirements for medical care. Even in developed countries, the additional costs for survivors can be substantial. For example, healthcare in infancy accounts for 75 percent of the $5.5–$6 billion in excess costs due to low birth weight in the United States (Lewit and others 1995). These healthcare costs differ according to the medical system, markets, and policies of a country. Costs during the neonatal period and infancy may be far less in low-income countries, where most births occur outside a clinical setting. But these lower medical costs associated with low birth weight come at the expense of higher mortality rates and worse outcomes for the survivors.

Impacts in Childhood

Children who are smaller than their peers because of prenatal nutritional deprivation risk many of the consequences that are noted for children with malnutrition in early life. Stunted children tend to start school later, progress through school less rapidly, have lower schooling attainment, and perform less well on cognitive achievement tests when they become older. Moreover, there is substantial evidence that the relationship between birth weight and cognitive function carries beyond the range of low birth weights into the range of normal birth weights (Matte and others 2001; Jefferis, Power, and Hertzman 2002; Richards and others 2002). Despite the absence of consensus on how much improvement there is in cognitive function as a child grows, many studies show that cognitive dysfunctions are moderated by social and economic factors (Jefferis, Power, and Hertzman 2002; Aylward 2003; Ment and others 2003). This underscores the call by Grantham-McGregor, Fernald, and Sethuraman (1999) for more studies of low birth weight in environments in which countervailing investments are not common, such as the low-income countries of interest here.

Low-birth-weight children require additional outpatient care and hospitalization during their childhood (Victora and others 1999). This has direct resource costs for healthcare services as well as lost time for uses including work and schooling for caregivers. As with health investments, increasing investments in education can mitigate a share of the long-term consequences of low birth weight for survivors. In developed countries, substantial resources are devoted to special education and social services (Petrou, Sach, and Davidson 2001). Where an education system does not recognize or cannot accommodate the individual needs of students, however, these costs are observed less as up-front costs during childhood than as the costs of reduced productivity in adulthood.

Impacts in Adulthood

There are at least three likely effects of low birth weight on adult outcomes.

First, adults who were born small are likely to have lower earnings and productivity because of lower cognitive achievement or stature (Strauss and Thomas 1998).

Second, fetal undernutrition at critical periods may result in permanent changes in body structure and metabolism. Even without subsequent nutritional insults, these changes can lead to increased probabilities of chronic noninfectious diseases later in life. This hypothesis is bolstered by studies that track low-birth-weight infants into their adult years and document increased susceptibility to coronary heart disease, non-insulin-dependent diabetes, high blood pressure, obstructive lung disease, high blood cholesterol, and renal damage (Barker 1998).

The evidence for this fetal origins hypothesis is still being assessed. At least two other explanations for the association between low birth weight and adult diseases have been offered. Low birth weight may be an indicator of poor socioeconomic status, which may have a causal impact on adult disease probabilities through other variables such as poor nutrition later in life or higher rates of smoking. If so, low birth weight may be only a correlate and not a causal variable. Low birth weight may be due to a genetic predisposition to insulin resistance, tending to account for a higher predisposition to adult diabetes and coronary heart diseases that reflects genetics rather than aspects of the uterine environment that may be influenced by medical and nutritional interventions. Without evaluating the evidence supporting or disputing the fetal origins hypothesis, this review shows what the implications of some estimated impacts would be in an economic context.

Third, low birth weight may have long-term consequences through transmission of the nutritional shock to the next generation. To the degree that stunted mothers have a higher probability of having low-birth-weight children, the biological and economic consequences of low birth weight may be perpetuated across generations.

Considerations in Measuring the Economic Benefits of Reducing the Incidence of Low Birth Weight

The economic benefits of reducing the incidence of low birth weight must be valued at prices that reflect the true marginal resource costs of those benefits. This statement has several implications.

First, many policies that reduce the incidence of low birth weight have multiple possible benefits. It is important that all be included so that the benefits are not undervalued.

Second, the benefits may be increases in some desirable outcome, such as schooling attainment, cognitive skills, and labor productivity, or reductions in costs, such as medical care costs associated with low birth weight.

Third, for each benefit, the causal contribution of low birth weight must be assessed with proper controls for measurement problems, background variables, and behavioral choices.

Fourth, if the impacts are not estimated in direct monetary terms, they must be translated into appropriate monetary terms for the context so that they can be summed across all the benefits to obtain the total. If prices are not available or are very distorted, an alternative is to use the resource cost of the cheapest alternative means of attaining the same objective (Summers 1994; Knowles and Behrman 2003).

Fifth, one of the most controversial steps in aggregating benefits is valuing a reduction in mortality. One approach in the literature is to value a life in accordance with an individual's expected discounted lifetime earnings. This approach is flawed, in part because it does not net out the costs of investments in that individual or of his or her consumption. More vexing, this approach values the life of an individual roughly in proportion to the per capita income of the society in which the individual is born. The alternative used here does not attempt to put a figure on the value of a life but only on the expected savings of resources in the society in which the low-birth-weight baby is born. That is, the savings in reducing mortality are estimated in the costs of other investments undertaken to reduce mortality (Summers 1994). This approach is sufficiently transparent that the assumption can be altered to assess how different assumptions would affect the overall estimated returns.

Sixth, the impacts are likely to occur over time, with different time paths for the impacts from different programs. Therefore, to make benefits comparable across programs, the present discounted values of benefits are generally used. Such calculations recognize that it is better to obtain a given monetary impact sooner rather than later, so that the money can be reinvested to earn further productive returns. This means, for example, that it is better to have a benefit from reducing the incidence of low birth weight that occurs quickly (reduced neonatal medical costs, for example) than one of equal monetary value that occurs decades later (reduced medical costs of the same magnitude from cardiovascular disease or diabetes later in life).

Lastly, many of the potential benefits come from reducing government expenditures, such as those for healthcare. As raising revenue generally incurs administrative costs and deadweight costs to the economy from economic distortions, the full economic cost of the expenditures is higher than the nominal value. This needs to be considered when valuing the reduction in the incidence of low birth weight and when considering programs to address the issue.

Empirical Evidence on the Economic Benefits of Reducing the Incidence of Low Birth Weight

Information on the economic benefits from reducing low birth weight is found not only in the nutritional, epidemiological, and biomedical literatures, but also in the socioeconomic and demographic literatures. The ideal is experimental data from randomized field designs that control for factors that determine both low birth weight and subsequent education, health, and productivity.

Although there are many randomized evaluations covering interventions that affect birth outcomes, only one such study was found in low-income countries, an experiment in Guatemala that also follows children into adulthood (Maluccio and others 2005).[2] Another set of studies tracks a cohort of children born at the end of the Dutch Hunger Winter—a short-term crisis caused by wartime rationing. Results from this natural experiment can be considered an outcome of an exogenous shock and thus considered to be relatively free of confounding factors. A similar natural shock was the famine in China between 1959 and 1961; recent research shows a doubling of rates of schizophrenia among the survivor cohort from that event (St. Clair and others 2005).

Additional information that controls for environmental factors is obtained from comparisons of twins (though the available studies are from developed countries). Although processes that lead to low birth weight among twins may be different from those among other children, in general weight differences in twins appear to reflect intrauterine resource competition.[3] Results from experimental evidence, twins studies, and cross-sectional studies are in general agreement, especially on the impact of birth weight on productivity.

Moreover, many studies show that outcomes are affected by birth weight even in the range of normal births. Thus unlike studies focused on prematurity, results tracking children born small for gestational age may reflect one end of a continuum that extends from low-birth-weight outcomes that are relatively common in some low-income countries (particularly in South Asia) to outcomes in developed countries for which there are more data. However, this does not imply that socioeconomic factors are not also important. Indeed, even in studies showing that the resources available in developed countries explain a larger share of the variance in cognitive development than does birth weight, birth weight still has a persistent and significant effect (Jefferis, Power, and Hertzman 2002).

Nonetheless, because information on many aspects of these processes is imperfect, simulations are explored under alternative assumptions to see how robust the estimates are to changes in some critical assumptions. And in recognition that benefits are context specific and vary across countries, representative price and resource cost structures typical of low-income countries are used rather than estimates specific to any country. Finally, the focus on reducing the incidence of low birth weight is mainly on crossing a threshold birth weight of 2,500 g, although many of the benefits carry over a continuum; only at relatively high birth weights do the benefits from increasing birth weight decline substantially (and possibly become negative).

As noted, accounting for the timing of the benefits is critical. The base case uses an assumed discount rate of 5 percent, but because of uncertainty regarding the appropriate discount rate, conclusions are tested for sensitivity to assumed discount

Table 1. Estimates of Present Discounted Values of Seven Major Benefits of Moving One Infant Out of Low-Birth-Weight Status, at Different Discount Rates (U.S. Dollars)

Benefits	3 percent	5 percent	10 percent
	Annual discount rate		
1. Reduced infant mortality	95	**99**	89
2. Reduced neonatal care	42	**42**	42
3. Reduced costs of infant and child illness	36	**35**	34
4. Productivity gain from reduced stunting	152	**85**	25
5. Productivity gain from increased cognitive ability	367	**205**	60
6. Reduced costs of chronic diseases	49	**15**	1
7. Intergenerational benefits	92	**35**	6
Total	832	**510**	257
Share of total at 5 percent discount rate (percent)	163	**100**	50

Note: The 5 percent discount rate, shown in boldface in the table, is the base case estimate.

Source: Authors' analysis based on data and assumptions described in the text.

rates. Data in table 1 compare the present discounted value of seven benefits from moving one infant from a low-birth-weight status at discount rates of 3, 5, and 10 percent.

In addition to the discounting of benefits received in the future, the timing of benefits during the life cycle is important because the probabilities are less than 1 that survivors of infancy will survive to the life-cycle stage at which various benefits arise. Thus not all the potential benefits from reduced illness and increased productivity will be realized. For all but the first two benefits (which focus on survival through infancy), the estimated benefits are adjusted for survival to the relevant age using World Health Organization life tables for India (www.who.int/countries/ind/en/), the country with the largest number of low-birth-weight babies. These life tables imply, for example, that the probabilities of surviving are 0.88 for age 20, 0.82 for age 40, and 0.66 for age 60. Thus the expected benefits from effects that are realized only later in the life cycle—such as lower costs for postinfancy diseases, higher birth weights in the next generation, greater productivity, and less chronic disease—are lower than they would be if, all else being equal, survival probabilities were higher.[4]

The following sections describe the empirical evidence on seven major economic benefits from reducing the incidence of low birth weight (the benefits are numbered and keyed to the summary benefits in table 1).

Reducing Infant Mortality

Several studies provide estimates of the probability of excess infant mortality for low-birth-weight infants. For example, a review of 12 data sets, including two from India and one from Guatemala, concludes that for infants born at term and weighing 2,000–2,499 g, the risk of neonatal death is 4 times that for infants weighing 2,500–2,999 g and 10 times that for infants weighing 3,000–3,499 g (Ashworth 1998). The risks of post-neonatal mortality are two and four times that of the other two groups. These studies did not control for socioeconomic variables, and a study that did so using data on twins to infer intrauterine resource competition—and, by inference, nutrition—found that an additional 400 g at birth in the United States led to a 14 percent decrease in mortality in the period between 28 days and 1 year for both fraternal and identical twins (Conley, Strully, and Bennett 2003). In contrast, in the first 28 days of life, an additional 400 g at birth led to a 27 percent decrease in the risk of mortality for fraternal twins compared with an 11 percent decrease for identical twins, implying a large role for genetic factors.

These risk ratios translate into fairly large differences in mortality rates, given the relatively high rates of low birth weight in many developing countries. The Indian and Guatemalan samples, for example, have neonatal morality rates of 21–39 per 1,000 live births and post-neonatal mortality rates of 25.3–60.0 per 1,000 neonatal survivors, with low birth weight in these samples of 21.2–39.0 percent. The mid-points of these ranges and of the percentage of low-birth-weight babies and considering the four-times greater risk of neonatal death for full-term infants weighing 2,000–2,499 g at birth and the two-times greater risk of post-neonatal death as for full-term infants weighing 2,500–2,999 g imply a drop of about 0.078 in the probability of an infant death (neonatal or post-neonatal) for each birth in the 2,500–2,999 g range instead of in the 2,000–2,499 g range.[5]

It is difficult to place a value on a life saved. Using a conservative estimate based on an $800 cost to save a life through measles immunization in the early 1990s (Summers 1994) and adjusting it for inflation in the next decade and for the distortion costs of raising these revenues yield an estimated alternative resource cost of saving an infant's life of about $1,250. Because not every low-birth-weight child dies, this value is multiplied by the excess probability that a low-birth-weight child would die in infancy, giving an estimated monetary benefit of reducing infant mortality associated with low birth weight of about $98. This benefit is obtained within a year or so of the assumed intervention occurring when the low-birth-weight baby is in the womb. Thus the discount rate does not greatly affect the present discounted value of this benefit (table 1, row 1).

Reducing the Additional Costs of Neonatal Medical Attention

The additional cost of neonatal medical care is the sum of extra hospital care and outpatient care required for low-birth-weight babies. Hospital care costs are the costs of a day of hospital stay times the number of additional days on average for babies born in hospitals and weighing less than 2,500 g. Under the assumption that these costs are incurred only for babies born in hospitals, the contribution of this component to the total may be small, even though the costs are not discounted over many years, because the share of children born in hospitals is small in most developing countries.

No reports of studies could be found that indicate the average length of hospital stay for low-birth-weight newborns compared with normal-weight newborns in low-income countries. On the basis of experience in Bangladesh, hospitalization is assumed to be 1–2 days for a normal-weight newborn with a normal delivery and 5–7 days for a low-birth-weight baby weighing between 1,500 and 2,500.[6] On the basis of a Tk2,000 per day cost at private hospitals, inclusive of medicine as the opportunity cost of care (government hospitals charge Tk200–300 plus medicine, but the cost of beds is subsidized), the extra direct hospital-related resource cost for a low-birth-weight newborn is $155, taken at the midpoints of the difference in days and using an exchange rate of Tk58 per dollar.

To this must be added the distortion costs from raising government revenues to finance the hospitalization and the cost of time to the parents for the extended hospital stay. Assuming that the distortion costs are about 25 percent ($39) of the hospitalization costs and that the time cost of the parents is $15, the total extra resource cost for the longer hospitalization for a low-birth-weight baby is $209. This is assumed to be incurred close enough to the intervention not to require discounting.

Most babies in low-income countries are born at home, not in hospitals. Although there may be some parallel costs for low-birth-weight babies born at home, they are likely to be much less than the costs of extra hospitalization. For the base estimates, therefore, 90 percent of babies are assumed to be born at home, and the additional resource costs for low-birth-weight babies born at home are estimated at 10 percent of that for low-birth-weight babies born in hospitals (table 1, row 2). Conservatively, the incremental costs of home care in the neonatal period are not considered. The methodology employed allows this—and any other component of the estimated benefits—to be varied to accommodate different conditions.

Reducing the Additional Costs of Subsequent Illnesses and Related Medical Care for Infants and Children

Several studies show a regular pattern of increased childhood illness for lower-birth-weight children, particularly in the first 2 years of life. For example, compared with normal-birth-weight children, low-birth-weight children 0–6 months old in Brazil have 33 percent more days with diarrhea, and low-birth-weight babies 0–59 months old in Papua New Guinea have 60 percent more (Ashworth 1998). In Brazil the increased days with diarrhea imply a doubling of the rate of hospitalization for dehydration and a 50 percent increase in hospitalization for pneumonia (Barros and others 1992). Similar increases in pneumonia and acute respiratory disease are observed for many countries (Victora and others 1999).

Such increased illness has direct and immediate costs plus indirect costs due to associated stunting. In the absence of published estimates of the resource costs of such illnesses and related medical care among low-birth-weight children, the additional total direct resource costs for the first 2 years of life are estimated at $40, at the center point of the end of the first year, with adjustment for the probability of surviving to 1 year old bringing the cost in the base case to $35 (table 1, row 3).

Discounted Lifetime Productivity Gain Due to Decreased Stunting

The gain in lifetime productivity from increasing the birth weight of a low-birth-weight baby to a normal weight has two components. The first can be derived from an estimate of the impact of low birth weight on adult height and from an estimate of the difference in earnings attributable to low stature, under the assumption that the impact on earnings reflects the impact on productivity. The second component, discussed in the subsequent section, stems from the effect of stature on the timing and attainment level of schooling (Alderman, Hoddinott, and Kinsey forthcoming). For both components, the estimates incorporate the probability of survival through the working years of adulthood for normal-weight babies.

Long-term follow-up studies in the United Kingdom indicate a loss of 0.5 standard deviations in height for children weighing an average of 1,000 g less at birth than normal-birth-weight controls (Strauss 2000). A study of identical twins in the United States found that a difference of 1,000 g in birth weight led to a 1.6 cm (roughly 1 percent) difference in adult height (Behrman and Rosenzweig 2004). In a randomized experimental study tracking a cohort of Guatemalan children whose mothers received supplementation, a 1 standard deviation difference in birth weight led to a 1.8 cm difference in adult height for males and a 0.6 cm difference for females (Li and others 2003).

What do differences of this magnitude mean for productivity? An estimate of the direct impact of adult height on wages for urban Brazil found that a 1 percent increase in height leads to a 2–2.4 percent increase in wages or earnings (Thomas and Strauss 1997). Although the Brazilian study uses sophisticated methodology to account for labor selectivity and joint determination of health, the result is similar to others reported in the literature. Indeed, height is even a significant explanatory variable for wages in the United States (Strauss and Thomas 1998). Results such as these—though admittedly about stunting in general and not necessarily stunting due to low birth weight—are used to infer the impact on productivity through reduced stunting. Increasing the birth weight of a low-birth-weight infant to above 2,500 g results in an expected benefit of about 2.2 percent of assumed annual earnings of $500 a year in constant prices over a work life from 15 to 60 years old (table 1, row 4).

Discounted Lifetime Productivity Gain Due to Increased Cognitive Ability

The indirect effect of height on wages mediated through schooling is likely to be even larger than the direct impact of height on wages. This indirect effect has been documented for preschool malnutrition. For example, a childhood shock that led to a 0.73 standard deviation decline in height in Zimbabwe resulted in a six-month delay in initiating enrollment and 0.8 years less of total schooling, leading to an estimated 14 percent reduction in lifetime earnings (Alderman, Hoddinott, and Kinsey forthcoming).

Learning may also be affected by the impairment of cognitive development that is associated with low birth weight, so reducing the incidence of low birth weight could also increase productivity through this channel. Two studies find that the cognitive impairment falls in a range of a 0.3–0.6 standard deviation decrease in intelligence quotient (IQ) (Sorensen and others 1997; Bhutta and others 2002). Extrapolation to the task at hand, however, is subject to several adjustments. These two studies investigate children whose birth weights reflect prematurity, whereas in low-income countries most low-birth-weight babies are a result of intrauterine growth retardation. Mental impairment may not be limited to extreme cases of low birth weight or to prematurity. One study found that intelligence scores continued to increase up to a birth weight of 4,200 g, with the difference between the low birth weight group and children born at 4,000 g being roughly 0.5 standard deviation of the score (Sorensen and others 1997). Another study comparing siblings with normal gestation found increases in IQ of similar magnitude with increases in birth weight (Matte and others 2001).

Next, the magnitude of impairment must be converted into an estimate of the impact on subsequent earnings. Two studies using the same data set but different measures of ability estimated the impact of IQ on earnings in the United States. One study shows that the logarithm of wages for men declined 0.05 with a 0.5 standard deviation decline in IQ, holding schooling constant (Altonji and Dunn 1996). This was slightly more than the impact of an additional year of postsecondary schooling. The other study modeled the influence of ability on schooling choice as well as on wage offers and found that a 0.5 standard deviation decline in cognitive ability led to a 8–12 percent decrease in wages (Cawley, Heckman, and Vytlacil 2001).

For Pakistan, a 0.5 standard deviation reduction in cognitive ability based on performance on Raven's matrices was found to result in a 6.5 percent reduction in wages (Alderman and others 1996). Similarly, for Kenya and Tanzania, Raven's scores influence schooling and learning conditional on years of school. Taking these pathways into account, a 0.5 standard deviation decline in ability would lead to declines in wages of 8 percent for Kenya and 5 percent for Tanzania (Boissiere, Knight, and Sabot 1985).[7]

Combined Productivity Gains from Decreased Stunting and Increased Cognitive Ability

An alternative approach to estimating the productivity gains from decreased incidence of low birth weight combines the fourth and fifth of the seven benefits considered in this article. It looks directly at individual earnings as a function of birth weight. Instead of summing the impact of low stature on wages and the impact of reduced cognitive function times an expectation of this type of impairment, the earnings of children with similar opportunities at birth but different birth weights can be compared. This approach, by drawing on a different set of studies using a different methodology, helps to narrow the plausible range of impact.

People 26 years old who were born small for gestational age (an average of 1,000 g less than the normal weight group) were found to earn 10 percent less than people of normal birth weights (Strauss 2000).[8] Difference in cognitive ability on standard tests ranged from 0.13 to 0.37 standard deviations in follow-up measurements between the ages of 5 and 16. Even with a modest difference in measured cognitive ability and no difference in average years of schooling, wages differed as much (even more) as they did under the assumption of a 0.5 standard deviation difference in cognitive ability or as derived from wage equations that include cognitive ability. In the United States, a 1,000 g difference in the birth weight of identical twins results in an 18.6 percent difference in wages as adults (Behrman and Rosenzweig 2004). A similar study of siblings found a much larger negative relation between low birth weight and the probability of completing high school than that found in cross-sectional estimates, though the use of siblings may confound low-birth-weight and genetic effects (Conley and Bennett 2000). Norwegian twins indicate that the long-run effects of birth weight on earnings are significant and similar to those found in cross-section (Black, Devereux, and Salvanes 2005). Another study finds that birth weight is negatively associated with rates of unemployment (Kristensen, Bjerkedal, and Irgens 2004).

Overall, considering either the total impact of low birth weight on wages or the sum of the impacts due to stunting, impaired cognitive development, and reduced schooling, the earnings impact of moving an infant out of a low birth weight status can be bracketed between 5 and 10 percent a year. The base estimate uses 7.5 percent. Taken together with the 2.2 percent expected productivity benefit from reduced stunting, this implies a 5.3 percent expected productivity benefit from improved ability. Again, annual earnings or productivity are assumed to be $500 in constant prices for a working life from 15 through 60 years old for those who survive to adulthood (see table 1, row 5).

Reduced Costs of Chronic Diseases Associated with Low Birth Weight

Numerous chronic illnesses are associated with fetal malnutrition, making it difficult to assign costs. Moreover, relatively few studies have traced the long-term impacts. As mentioned, fetal malnutrition may affect adult health in ways that low birth weight does not, for example, by influencing gene expression. Moreover, what effect low birth weight has on chronic disease may depend on other deprivations in the individual's life, adding another dimension to any assumptions made. And, again because information is lacking on how many low birth weight children will survive to the ages at which chronic diseases are likely to strike, adjustments are made for survival probabilities using Indian life tables.

One study that attempts to calculate the costs of the impacts of low birth weight and of subsequent nutritional and dietary patterns on chronic disease considers the cost of diet-related chronic disease in two economies—China and Sri Lanka (Popkin, Horton, and Kim 2001). All diet-related factors were estimated to account for costs totaling 2.1 percent of GNP in 1995 in China and 0.3 percent in Sri Lanka. For both countries the costs were projected to rise appreciably over the next generation. The methodology used in these studies differs from that used here in at least two respects. First, the costs are estimates for the economy, not per low birth weight averted. Second, the average loss of earnings (assumed to be 10 years per adult death) is discounted only to the year of death, not from the year of the presumed interventions that might affect low birth weight, as is done here.

The basic estimates in the current study make two broad assumptions. First, the cost of lost productivity and increased medical care is assumed to be equivalent to 10 years of earnings in a low-income population ($5,000) and to be experienced on average at age 60. Second, the probability of experiencing these chronic diseases is assumed to be reduced by 0.087 for moving a baby out of the low birth weight status.[9]

Reduction in Intergenerational Impacts

Since many women begin having children in their teens or early twenties, some of the costs for the second generation of low birth weight babies may occur before all of the direct costs for the earlier generation have been realized, such as the costs of chronic illnesses in adults who were themselves low birth weight babies. Of course, preventing such intergenerational impacts affects only women who survive to childbearing age.

Not much persuasive evidence was found on the impact of mother's low birth weight on the birth weight of her children. For the United States, in studies of identical twins, the significant positive correlation disappears if all endowments are controlled for (Behrman and Rosenzweig 2004). In low-income rural Guatemala an experimental design at the community level found evidence of an intergenerational effect for nutritional supplements (Ramakrishnan and others 1999). Therefore, benefits are estimated under several assumptions (see table 1, row 7). First, these effects are only for mothers who were low birth weight babies, not fathers, and thus apply to about half of low birth weight babies. Second, on average, these mothers have four children, born when the mother is 17, 20, 26, and 35. Third, for a mother who was a low-birth-weight baby, the probability for each of her children of being low birth weight is 1 in 5. Fourth, this probability is reduced to 1 in 10 if the mother was not a low birth weight baby. And lastly, the benefits of reducing the incidence of low birth weight for the next generation of children over their life cycle are the same as the benefits for the mothers, but lagged in time and therefore discounted more, over three generations of children.[10]

Summary of Benefits from Moving One Infant Out of Low-Birth-Weight Status

The total estimate of the present discounted value (at the 5 percent basic discount rate) per infant born at normal weight rather than low birth weight is about $510. In purely economic terms that means that it would be desirable to reduce the incidence of low birth weight infants in low-income populations as long as the true resource cost of doing so is less than $510 per affected infant.

In these estimates the overall benefits are dominated by the benefits of increased productivity from reducing stunting and improving cognitive ability (working in part through the effects on schooling). These two benefits account for more than half (57 percent) of the total. While these benefits emerge only after considerable delay and are received only by those who survive to working ages, they persist over an individual's working life. Thus their effects are considerable even when discounted at 5 percent from the time of the intervention.

Though the estimated benefits from reduced infant mortality and reduced costs of neonatal care and infant and child illnesses are not huge, their contribution is appreciable because the benefits occur very early in the life cycle and are not discounted very much. In contrast, the present discounted value of the reduction in the costs of chronic diseases is fairly small (3 percent) because of the discounting and the survival probabilities, even though the constant dollar values per year are fairly large at the time they occur.

Sensitivity of Basic Estimates of the Benefits of Reducing the Incidence of Low Birth Weight to Selected Critical Assumptions

The illustrative estimates in table 1 are conditional on many assumptions and a few informed guesses. This section examines how sensitive the estimates are to some of these assumptions and guesses.

Discount Rates

The basic estimates use a real discount rate of 5 percent. Changing the discount rate to 10 percent results in an overall present discounted value of benefits half that obtained with the 5 percent discount rate. Changing it to 3 percent increases benefits by 163 percent (see table 1).

The present discounted values of all benefits (except reduced neonatal care, which is not discounted) decline as the discount rate increases, but at very different rates. The benefits that are realized early in the life cycle—reduced infant mortality, reduced neonatal care, and reduced costs of infant and child illness—become relatively more important, accounting for 20 percent of the present discounted value of total benefits at a discount rate of 3 percent, 33 percent at a discount rate of 5 percent, and 64 percent at a discount rate of 10 percent. Figure 1 shows a similar perspective on the differences in the shares of total estimated present discounted value attributable to individual benefits for six different discount rates. (The figure does not indicate that the totals change, only the changes in shares.)

Changes in Estimates of Individual Benefits

Benefits will vary with country-specific conditions. For example, a greater share of babies born in hospitals and higher costs of medical care will increase the benefit from reduced neonatal care, while higher average productivity will increase the benefits from productivity gains. To illustrate the implications of these uncertainties and the differences across countries, simulations were conducted starting with the base estimates with a 5 percent discount rate but increasing each of the seven benefits in turn by 50 percent (table 2). For example, the simulations show what would happen if the probability of infant mortality fell by 0.117 instead of by 0.078.

The total present discounted value of benefits increases from the base estimate of $510 to $517 for reduced chronic illnesses to $612 for the productivity effects of increased cognitive ability. Thus under each of these alternatives, somewhat higher cost interventions would be warranted. These simulations also illustrate that it is much more important to pin down some of the benefits than others. With a 5 percent discount rate it would be more important to lessen the uncertainty about impacts on economic productivity and then on the costs of illness and death early in life than about the costs and probabilities of chronic diseases. With a higher discount rate, the value of improved estimates would shift somewhat toward events earlier in the life cycle, while with a lower discount rate the shift would be toward events later in the life cycle.

Any of the assumptions used in the estimates could be varied to explore the effects of variations in the core assumptions in a manner parallel to that illustrated here, including reducing rather than increasing assumed benefits.

Linking to Interventions Related to Low Birth Weight

One practical use of the benefits estimated here would be to adapt the cost structure to a particular environment and compare the expected discounted benefit with the cost of an intervention per low birth weight prevented. While this article does not

Figure 1. Composition of Total Present Discounted Values by Seven Classes of Benefits from Moving One Infant Out of Low Birth Weight Status, at Different Discount Rates

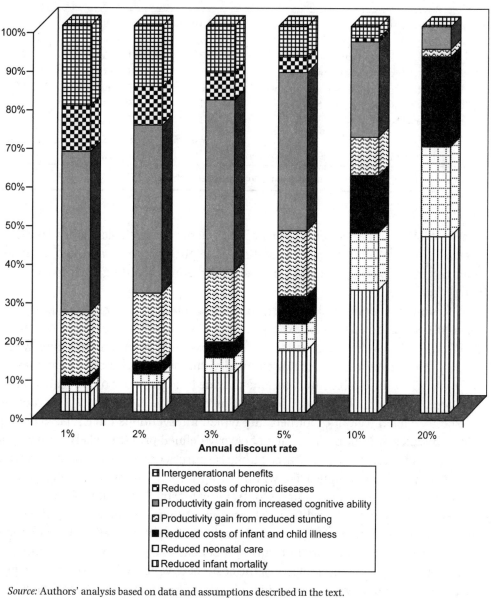

Intergenerational benefits
Reduced costs of chronic diseases
Productivity gain from increased cognitive ability
Productivity gain from reduced stunting
Reduced costs of infant and child illness
Reduced neonatal care
Reduced infant mortality

Source: Authors' analysis based on data and assumptions described in the text.

attempt to derive consensus estimates of the costs of different interventions, it is nonetheless useful to consider some illustrative examples.

Many interventions have been proposed to address low-birth-weight problems (Merialdi and others 2003; Steketee 2003; Alderman and Behrman 2004), including

Table 2. Impact of Increasing Each Benefit One at a Time by 50 Percent Relative to Estimates in Table 1, at 5 Percent Discount Rate (U.S. dollars)

Benefits	1	2	3	4	5	6	7
1. Reduced infant mortality	**139**	93	93	93	93	93	93
2. Reduced neonatal care	42	**63**	42	42	42	42	42
3. Reduced costs of infant and child illness	35	35	**53**	35	35	35	35
4. Productivity gain from reduced stunting	85	85	85	**128**	85	85	85
5. Productivity gain from increased cognitive ability	205	205	205	205	**308**	205	205
6. Reduced costs of chronic diseases	15	15	15	15	15	**23**	15
7. Intergenerational benefits	35	35	35	35	35	35	**53**
Total	556	531	528	552	612	517	527
Share of total in table 1 at 5 percent discount rate (percent)	109	104	103	108	120	101	103

Source: Authors' analysis based on data and assumptions described in the text.

antimicrobial treatments, antiparasitic treatments, insecticide-treated bednets, maternal health records to track gestational weight gain, iron and folate supplements, targeted food supplements, and social marketing regarding birth spacing and timing of marriage.

While some recommended interventions focus solely on low birth weight, some address other goals as well—for example, campaigns against smoking or consumption of other drugs during pregnancy. To assess such interventions, one would ideally sum the expected present discounted value of all anticipated outcomes. In reality, most lists of possible interventions provide little guidance on priorities, either for using scarce public resources for the general purpose of alleviating problems related to low birth weight or for deciding which interventions have relatively high returns in which situations. This lack of clearly defined priorities likely reduces the influence of advocates of using scarce public resources to alleviate problems related to low birth weight. And it also likely impedes agreement among advocates on how to use any additional public resources for treating low birth weight problems.

Under the assumptions used to construct the estimates in table 1, any intervention that costs less than $510 per case of low birth weight averted in a low-income country is a suitable candidate in terms of a benefit to cost ratio greater than 1.[11] Rouse (2003) presents a brief review of the cost-effectiveness of interventions to prevent adverse pregnancy outcomes, including low birth weight. He indicates, for example, that it costs $46 per case of low birth weight averted with treatments for asymptomatic sexually transmitted bacterial infections, where these are prevalent. Even taking into account the costs of raising revenue for such an intervention, costs of this magnitude are far lower than the benefits summarized in table 1.

As another example, consider an extensive field trial of supplementation with iron and folate in a community in Nepal where rates of low birth weight and anemia are both high. Christian and others (2003) found that 11 women would need to be reached with the micronutrient supplements to prevent one case of low birth weight. While no cost data were provided in the published study, Christian and West (2003) in a personal communication estimated that the costs of the experimental program of $64 per pregnant woman reached could be reduced to $13 in an ongoing program. With just 1 in 11 births benefiting directly in terms of a case of low birth weight averted, the initial cost does not represent an economically efficient intervention. However, if at least one-third of the estimated cost reduction for an ongoing program can be realized, the intervention would be economically efficient. Moreover, economies of scope would allow the provision of vitamin A supplementation at little marginal cost and thus might reduce both infant and maternal mortality.

Concluding Comments

This review demonstrates that the economic benefits from reducing the incidence of low birth weight in low-income countries may be fairly substantial. Under plausible assumptions each infant moved out of low birth weight status would result in $510 in benefits. Thus there may be many interventions that are warranted purely on the grounds of saving resources or increasing productivity. With a 5 percent discount rate, the gains are estimated to come primarily from increases in labor productivity (partly through more education), with the gains from avoiding costs due to infant illness and death second in importance. The beneficiaries of these gains are largely people who would otherwise be poor. If the appropriate discount rate is higher than 5 percent, then the relative gains from reduced illness and death in infancy would increase while those from increased productivity would decline.

In contrast, the estimated gains from reducing chronic diseases, a topic of considerable interest in recent years, are comparatively small for any reasonable discount rate. That is so because the gains—even if large when realized—occur decades after any resource-using interventions that might reduce the incidence of low birth weight.

Still, much remains unknown or poorly known. Better estimates are needed of the individual effects, particularly those that are relatively large for reasonable discount rates (those related directly to productivity and to early life-cycle benefits), and of the discount rates themselves. There would also be gains from understanding more about the impacts of incremental changes in birth weight rather than just the standard dichotomy of low birth weight (below 2,500 g) or not.

While improving birth weights clearly contributes to equity—low birth weight babies are concentrated among low-income households, and poor health is a facet of any multidimensional view of poverty—not enough is known about the efficiency rationale for public investments. Estimates that distinguish private and social gains from reducing the incidence of low birth weight could help in assessing the efficiency case for public subsidies. Also helpful would be more information on the market failures that prevent private individuals from capturing all or some of the potential returns. A priori it would appear that the positive externalities from reducing the incidence of low birth weight—and therefore the potential efficiency gains—vary considerably across the impacts considered here. Reducing infant and childhood infectious diseases seems to have relatively high externalities. Similarly, large positive externalities are often claimed for learning, and so there should be gains to increasing cognitive skills. But despite such claims, little is known about the magnitudes of these possible externalities.

These and other improvements in knowledge would strengthen the informational basis for making policies related to low birth weight. The estimates presented here based on available information suggest that reducing the incidence of low birth weight in low-income countries might well provide substantial economic gains.

Notes

Harold Alderman is a lead human development economist in the Africa Region of the World Bank; his e-mail address is halderman@worldbank.org. Jere R. Behrman is the William R. Kenan Jr Professor of Economics and a research associate of the Population Studies Center, University of Pennsylvania; his e-mail address is jbehrman@econ.upenn.edu. This study was funded in part by grants from the National Institutes of Health (NIH/Fogarty TW-05598) and the National Science Foundation (NSF SES 0136616). The authors thank Shanta Devarajan, John Fiedler, John Hoddinott, Susan Horton, Reynaldo Martorell, Mohammed Shahjahan, and three anonymous referees for useful advice received during the preparation of this article.

1. This type of intervention has proven effective even among nonanemic African-American women in the United States (Cogswell and others 2003).

2. The study provides estimates of the intergenerational impacts of low birth weight. While there are preliminary estimates from the study that also indicate significant impacts from a nutritional intervention for a poor population 6–24 months old on earnings at 25–42 years old, the impact of low birth weight on this cohort has not yet been analyzed.

3. See Behrman and Rosenzweig (2004) for a discussion on whether estimates from twins can be generalized to broader populations.

4. This adjustment for survival probabilities was not used in a previous version of this study (Alderman and Behrman 2004), and thus the estimated benefits in the current study are slightly lower (about 10 percent) than without the adjustments.

5. The midpoint of the neonatal death rate (30.1) is assumed to be the weighted average of low birth weight and normal-birth-weight infants. All low birth weights are assumed to be in the 2,000–2,499 g range and all normal birth weights in the 2,500–2,999 g range. Given the fourfold greater risk of neonatal death for the low birth weight babies, this implies a neonatal mortality rate of 61.0 for low birth weight infants and 15.2 for normal-birth-weight infants, so the difference is 45.8 or a probability of 0.046. A parallel calculation for the twofold greater risk of post-neonatal death among neonatal survivors with an overall mortality rate at the midpoint of 42.7 and a midpoint of the birth weight range of 32.5 implies that the post-neonatal mortality rate is 64.4 for low birth weight infants and 32.2 for normal-birth-weight infants, so the difference is 32.2 or a probability of 0.032. Together these calculations

imply that a shift from low birth weight to normal-birth-weight status reduces the probability of mortality in such a population by about 0.078.

6. The authors are indebted to Dr Mohammed Shahjahan of the Micronutrient Initiative and former Medical Director of Save the Children Foundation's Children's Nutrition Unit in Dhaka for this information.

7. Additional results covering Chile, Colombia, and Ghana are reviewed in Alderman and Behrman (2004).

8. Small for gestational age is not identical to intrauterine growth retardation, but intrauterine growth retardation is often used as a proxy for small for gestational age when gestational age is not known precisely.

9. The reasoning behind this approximation is as follows. For the stereotypical low-income developing country, about 10 percent of adult deaths are considered to be due to these diseases under the assumption that the eventual share of deaths from these causes will be the same as the annual share of deaths. About 15 percent of the adult population is assumed to have been of low birth weight (much higher than in China and many low-income countries, but lower than in many low-income countries in South Asia and Sub-Saharan Africa), and the odds ratio of having these chronic diseases is twice as high for those who were low birth weight as for those who were not. Then let X be the probability of having these chronic diseases for normal-birth-weight babies (and $2X$ for low birth weight babies), where $X = 8.7$ percent is the solution to 10 percent $= 0.85X + 0.15 (2X)$. Since the odds ratio for adults who were low birth weight babies is twice that for adults who were not, the reduction in the probability of having these chronic diseases by moving a baby from low birth weight to normal-birth-weight status is 0.087.

10. The impact of reduced schooling or lower cognitive ability on nutrition in the second generation is not included, although the impact of schooling on nutrition is well known, and recent evidence confirms the impact of cognitive ability as well (Rubalcava and Teruel 2004).

11. As costs and benefits occur in the same locality, exchange rates and purchasing power parity essentially net out in the estimates of benefit–cost ratios.

References

Alderman, Harold, Jere Behrman, David Ross, and Richard Sabot. 1996. "The Returns to Endogenous Human Capital in Pakistan's Rural Wage Labor Market." *Oxford Bulletin of Economics and Statistics* 58(1):29–55.

Alderman, Harold, John Hoddinott, and Bill Kinsey. Forthcoming. "Long Term Consequences of Early Childhood Malnutrition." *Oxford Economic Papers*.

Alderman, Harold, and Jere Behrman. 2004. "Estimated Economic Benefits of Reducing Low Birth Weight in Low-Income Countries." HNP Discussion Paper. World Bank, Washington, D.C.

Allen, Lindsay, and Stuart Gillespie. 2001. "What Works? A Review of Efficacy and Effectiveness of Nutrition Interventions." Nutrition and Development Series 5. Asian Development Bank, Manila.

Altonji, Joseph, and Thomas Dunn. 1996. "The Effects of Family Characteristics on the Returns to Education." *Review of Economics and Statistics* 78(4):692–704.

Ashworth, A. 1998. "Effects of Intrauterine Growth Retardation on Mortality and Morbidity in Infants in Young Children." *European Journal of Clinical Nutrition* 52(81):S34–42.

Aylward, Glen. 2003. "Cognitive Function in Preterm Infants: No Simple Answers." *Journal of the American Medical Association* 289(6):747–50.

Barker, D. J. P. 1998. *Mothers, Babies, and Health in Later Life*, 2nd ed. London: Churchill Livingstone.

Barros, F. C., S. R. Huttly, C. G. Victora, B. R. Kirkwood, and J. P. Vaughan. 1992. "Comparisons of Causes and Consequences of Prematurity and Interuterine Growth Retardation: A Longitudinal Study in Southern Brazil." *Pediatrics* 90(2):238–44.

Behrman, Jere, and Mark Rosenzweig. 2004. "The Returns to Birth Weight." *Review of Economics and Statistics* 86(2):586–601.

Bhutta, Adnan, Mario Cleves, Patrick Casey, Mary Cradock, and K. J. Anand. 2002. "Cognitive and Behavioral Outcomes of School-Aged Children Who Were Born Preterm." *Journal of the American Medical Association* 288(6):728–37.

Black, Sandra, Paul Devereux, and Kjell Salvanes. 2005. "From the Cradle to the Labor Market? The Effect of Birth Weight on Adult Outcomes." University of California, LA.

Boissiere, Maurice, John B. Knight, and Richard H. Sabot. 1985. "Earnings, Schooling, Ability, and Cognitive Skills." *American Economic Review* 75(5):1016–30.

Cawley, John, James Heckman, and Edward Vytlacil. 2001. "Three Observations on Wages and Measured Cognitive Ability." *Labor Economics* 8(4):419–42.

Christian, Parul, Subarna Khatry, Joanne Katz, Elizabeth Pardhan, Steven LeClerq, Sharada Shrestha, Ramesh Adhikari, Alfred Sommer, and Keith West. 2003. "Effects of Alternative Maternal Micronutrient Supplements on Low Birth Weight in Rural Nepal: Double Blind Randomised Community Trial." *British Medical Journal* 326(7389):571–4.

Cogswell, Mary E., Ibrahim Parvanta, Liza Ickes, Ray Yip, and Gary M. Brittenham. 2003. "Iron Supplementation during Pregnancy, Anemia, and Birth Weight: A Randomized Controlled Trial." *American Journal of Clinical Nutrition* 78(4):773–81.

Conley, Dalton, Kate Strully, and Neil Bennett. 2003. "A Pound of Flesh or Just Proxy? Using Twin Differences to Estimate the Effects of Birth Weight on (Literal) Life Chances." NBER Working Paper 9901. National Bureau of Economic Research, Cambridge, MA.

Conley, Dalton, and Neil G. Bennett. 2000. "Is Biology Destiny? Birth Weight and Life Chances." *American Sociological Review* 65(3):458–67.

Grantham-McGregor, S., L. Fernald, and K. Sethuraman. 1999. "Effects of Health and Nutrition on Cognitive and Behavioural Development in Children in the First Three Years of Life. Part 1. Low Birth Weight, Breastfeeding, and Protein-Energy Malnutrition." *Food and Nutrition Bulletin* 20(1):53–75.

Horton, Susan. 1999. "Opportunities for Investments in Nutrition in Low-Income Asia." *Asian Development Review* 17(1&2):246–73.

Horton, Susan, and Jay Ross. 2003. "The Economics of Iron Deficiency." *Food Policy* 28(1):51–75.

Jamison, D., H. Mosley, A. Measham, and J. Bobadilla, eds. 1993. *Disease Control Priorities in Developing Countries.* Oxford: Oxford University Press. Available online at www.fic.nih.gov/dcpp/dcp2.html.

Jefferis, Barbara, Chris Power, and Clyde Hertzman. 2002. "Birth Weight, Childhood Socioeconomic Environment, and Cognitive Development in the 1958 British Birth Cohort Study." *British Medical Journal* 325(7359):305–8.

Knowles, James, and Jere R. Behrman. 2003. "Assessing the Economic Returns to Investing in Youth in Developing Countries." World Bank, Human Development Network, Washington, D.C.

Kramer, M. 1998. "Socioeconomic Determinants of Intrauterine Growth Retardation." *European Journal of Clinical Nutrition* 52(81):S29–33.

Kristensen, Petter, Tor Bjerkedal, and Lorentz Irgens. 2004. "Birthweight and Work Participation in Adulthood." *International Journal of Epidemiology* 33(4):849–56.

Lewit, E., L. Baker, H. Corman, and P. Shiono. 1995. "The Direct Costs of Low Birth Weight." *Future of Children* 5(1):35–56.

Li, Haojie, Aryeh Stein, Huiman Barhhart, Usha Ramakrishnan, and Reynaldo Martorell. 2003. "Associations between Prenatal and Postnatal Growth and Adult Body Size and Composition." *American Journal of Clinical Nutrition* 77(6):1498–505.

Maluccio, John A., John Hoddinott, Jere R. Behrman, Agnes Quisumbing, Reynaldo Martorell, and Aryeh D. Stein. 2005. "The Impact of an Experimental Nutritional Intervention in Childhood on Education among Guatemalan Adults." Philadelphia, Washington, D.C. and Atlanta: University of Pennsylvania, International Food Policy Research Institute and Emory University.

Matte, T., M. Bresnahan, M. Begg, and E. Susser. 2001. "Influence of Variation in Birth Weight within Normal Range and within Sibships on IQ at Age 7 Years: Cohort Study." *British Medical Journal* 323(7308):310–4.

Ment, Laura, Betty Vohr, Walther Allan, Karol Katz, Karen Schneider, Michael Westerveld, Charles Duncan, and Robert Makuch. 2003. "Change in Cognitive Function over Time in Very Low Birth Weight Infants." *Journal of the American Medical Association* 289(6):705–11.

Merialdi, Mario, Guillermo Carroli, Jose Villar, Edgardo Abalosi, Metin Gulmezoglu, Regina Kulier, and Mercedes de Onis. 2003. "Nutritional Interventions during Pregnancy for the Prevention or Treatment of Impaired Fetal Growth: An Overview of Randomized Controlled Trials." *Journal of Nutrition* 133(5):S1626–31.

Petrou, Stavros, T. Sach, and L. Davidson. 2001. "The Long-term Costs of Preterm Birth and Low Birth Weight: Results of a Systematic Review." *Child Care, Health, and Development* 27(2):97–115.

Popkin, Barry, Susan Horton, and Soowon Kim. 2001. "The Nutritional Transition and Diet-Related Chronic Disease in Asia: Implications for Prevention." FCND Discussion Paper 105. International Food Policy Research Institute, Washington, D.C.

Ramakrishnan, U., R. Martorell, D. Schroeder, and R. Flores. 1999. "Intergenerational Effects on Linear Growth." *Journal of Nutrition* 129(2):544–9.

Richards, M., R. Hardy, D. Kuh, and M. Wadsworth. 2002. "Birth Weight, Postnatal Growth, and Cognitive Function in a National UK Birth Cohort." *International Journal of Epidemiology* 31(2):342–8.

Rouse, Dwight. 2003. "Potential Cost-Effectiveness of Nutrition Interventions to Prevent Adverse Pregnancy Outcomes in the Developing World." *Journal of Nutrition* 133(5):S1640–44.

Rubalcava, Luis, and Graciela Teruel. 2004. "The Role of Maternal Schooling, Cognitive Ability, and Public Determinants on Child Health." *Economics and Human Biology* 2(3):439–56.

Sorensen, H., S. Sabroc, J. Olsen, K. Rothman, M. Gillman, and P. Fischer. 1997. "Birth Weight and Cognitive Function in Young Adult Life: Historical Cohort Study." *British Medical Journal* 315(7133):401–3.

St. Clair, David, and others. 2005. "Rates of Adult Schizophrenia Following Prenatal Exposure to the Chinese Famine of 1959–1961." *Journal of the American Medical Association* 294(5):557–62.

Steketee, Richard. 2003. "Pregnancy, Nutrition, and Parasitic Disease." *Journal of Nutrition* 133(5):S1661–67.

Strauss, John, and Duncan Thomas. 1998. "Health, Nutrition, and Economic Development." *Journal of Economic Literature* 36(2):766–817.

Strauss, Richard, S. 2000. "Adult Functional Outcome of Those Born Small for Gestational Age." *Journal of the American Medical Association* 283(5):625–32.

Summers, Lawrence H. 1994. "Investing in All the People: Educating Women in Developing Countries." EDI Seminar Paper 45. World Bank, Economic Development Institute, Washington, D.C.

Thomas, Duncan, and John Strauss. 1997. "Health and Wages: Evidence on Men and Women in Urban Brazil." *Journal of Econometrics* 77(1):159–87.

UN SCN (United Nations System Sub-Committee on Nutrition). 2004. *5th Report on the World Nutrition Situation: Nutrition for Improved Development Outcomes.* New York.

Verhoeff, F. H., B. J. Brabin, S. van Buuren, L. Chimsuku, P. Kazembe, J. M. Wit, and R. L. Broadhead. 2001. "An Analysis of Intra-uterine Growth Retardation in Rural Malawi." *European Journal of Clinical Nutrition* 55(8):682–9.

Victora, Cesar, Betty Kirkwood, Ann Ashworth, Robert Black, Stephen Rogers, Sunil Sazawal, Harry Campbell, and Sandy Gore. 1999. "Potential Interventions for the Prevention of Childhood Pneumonia in Developing Countries: Improving Nutrition." *American Journal of Clinical Nutrition* 70(3):309–20.

Villar, J., and J. M. Belizán. 1982. "The Relative Contribution of Prematurity and Fetal Growth Retardation to Low Birth Weight in Developing and Developed Societies." *American Journal of Obstetrics and Gynecology* 143(7):793–8.

Choosing a System of Unemployment Income Support: Guidelines for Developing and Transition Countries

Milan Vodopivec

Mounting evidence suggests that excessive job protection reduces employment and labor market flows, hinders technological innovations, pushes workers into the informal sector, and hurts vulnerable groups by depriving them of job opportunities. Flexible labor markets stimulate job creation, investment, and growth, but they create job insecurity and displace some workers. How can the costs of such insecurity and displacements be minimized while ensuring that the labor market remains flexible? Each of the main unemployment income support systems (unemployment insurance, unemployment assistance, unemployment insurance savings accounts, severance pay, and public works) has strengths and weaknesses. Country-specific conditions—chief among them labor market and other institutions, the capacity to administer each type of system, and the size of the informal sector—determine which system is best suited to developing and transition countries.

This article evaluates five systems of unemployment income support, identifying the key strengths and weaknesses of each system, assessing the applicability of each system to developing and transition counties, and drawing lessons about the design of income support systems. Two sets of criteria are used to judge the desirability of each type of system in a particular country. Performance criteria assess how well a system typically works—how well it protects workers' incomes and how it affects efficiency and income distribution. Design and implementation criteria assess how suitable a system is in a particular country given the country-specific conditions.

To evaluate the desirability of a particular income support system, the article examines theoretical and empirical insights about its performance and examines how the prevailing conditions in developing and transition countries are likely to affect its functioning. This pragmatic approach is used to supplement the findings of economic models, which can provide only partial guidance for policymakers in

doi:10.1093/wbro/lkj003   Advance Access publication 14 February 2006   21:49–89

developing and transition countries, because implicit assumptions of theoretical modeling (such as the existence of suitable institutional capacity and strict enforcement of law and order) often do not apply.

What Are the Options?

Policymakers can choose among various income support systems for the unemployed. Five systems are examined here: unemployment insurance, unemployment assistance, unemployment insurance savings accounts, severance pay, and public works.

Unemployment Insurance

Unemployment insurance (together with pension and health insurance) is provided as part of social insurance. The system typically requires that workers and their employers pay earnings-related contributions that, upon separation, entitle workers to unemployment benefits according to predetermined eligibility conditions. While it mimics market insurance, the system deviates from actuarial principles by charging premiums that do not reflect individual risks. To qualify for benefits, a worker must satisfy the minimum covered employment or contribution requirement. The cause of dismissal may affect the individual's eligibility for benefits, with workers who quit their jobs often disqualified. Continuing eligibility requires that applicants be available for jobs, actively search for them, and be willing to accept them. Benefits are typically determined by the replacement rate—the proportion of the individual's pay in the most recent employment spell. The initial replacement rate is usually 40–75 percent. If provided, unemployment insurance is mandatory in developed countries, where it is the most widely used income protection system for the unemployed, typically covering all workers (table 1).

Why is unemployment insurance provided by the public and not the private sector? The market fails to provide unemployment insurance primarily because of significant information asymmetries, which give rise to "moral hazard" and adverse selection problems that cannot be handled by private providers (moral hazard arises because unemployment insurance reduces self-protection; adverse selection arises because information problems prevent insurers from charging higher premiums to poor risks). Correcting for market failures calls not only for regulation—obligatory membership to avoid adverse selection—but also for its public provision, to improve monitoring capacity. Another advantage of publicly providing unemployment insurance is the enhanced ability to pool resources across large groups, which reduces strains on the system arising from the covariant nature of unemployment risk. Moreover, financial backing by the government is often provided when the system faces financial difficulties.

Table 1. Unemployment Support Systems, by Country

Country	Unemployment Insurance[a] Replacement Rate (Percent of Individual's Pre-unemployment Wage where not Indicated Otherwise)	Unemployment Insurance[a] Maximum Duration (Months)	Unemployment Assistance[a] Replacement Rate	Unemployment Assistance[a] Maximum Duration (Months)	Unemployment Insurance Savings Accounts Replacement Rate (Percent of Individual's Pre-unemployment Wage)	Unemployment Insurance Savings Accounts Potential Duration	Unemployment Insurance Savings Accounts Contribution Rate (Employer + Worker Obligation)	Severance Pay[b] (Benefits) After 20 Years of Service	Public Works[c] Participation Rates	Public Works[c] Expenditure as Percent of GDP	Reference Variables Unemployment Rate[d]	Reference Variables Share of Informal Employment[e]
Low-income countries												
Afghanistan	n.a.	n.a.	n.a.	n.a.	n.a.	n.a.	n.a.	n.a.	—	—	—	n.a.
Angola	n.a.	n.a.	n.a.	n.a.	n.a.	n.a.	n.a.	n.a.	—	—	—	n.a.
Armenia	$4–$7	12	n.a.	n.a.	n.a.	n.a.	n.a.	2	—	—	22.9	26.7
Azerbaijan	70%	6	n.a.	n.a.	n.a.	n.a.	n.a.	4	—	—	1	—
Bangladesh	n.a.	n.a.	n.a.	n.a.	n.a.	n.a.	n.a.	9.3	0.2	—	**2.5**	—
Benin	n.a.	n.a.	n.a.	n.a.	n.a.	n.a.	n.a.	n.a.	—	—	—	—
Burkina Faso	n.a.	n.a.	n.a.	n.a.	n.a.	n.a.	n.a.	n.a.	—	—	—	65
Burundi	n.a.	n.a.	n.a.	n.a.	n.a.	n.a.	n.a.	n.a.	—	—	—	n.a.
Cambodia	n.a.	n.a.	n.a.	n.a.	n.a.	n.a.	n.a.	n.a.	—	—	**2.2**	n.a.
Cameroon	n.a.	n.a.	n.a.	n.a.	n.a.	n.a.	n.a.	6.75	—	—	—	—
Central African Rep.	n.a.	n.a.	n.a.	n.a.	n.a.	n.a.	n.a.	n.a.	n.a.	n.a.	—	n.a.
Chad	n.a.	n.a.	n.a.	n.a.	n.a.	n.a.	n.a.	n.a.	n.a.	n.a.	—	n.a.
China	Flat (set below minimum wage)	12–24	n.a.	n.a.	n.a.	n.a.	n.a.	20	—	—	3	21.9
Congo, Dem. Rep. of	n.a.	n.a.	n.a.	n.a.	n.a.	n.a.	n.a.	n.a.	n.a.	n.a.	—	n.a.
Congo, Rep. of	n.a.	n.a.	n.a.	n.a.	n.a.	n.a.	n.a.	n.a.	n.a.	n.a.	—	n.a.
Côte D'Ivoire	n.a.	n.a.	n.a.	n.a.	n.a.	n.a.	n.a.	6.8	n.a.	n.a.	—	—
Ethiopia	n.a.	n.a.	n.a.	n.a.	n.a.	n.a.	n.a.	9.3	1	—	—	—
Gambia, The	n.a.	n.a.	n.a.	n.a.	n.a.	n.a.	n.a.	n.a.	n.a.	n.a.	11.9	—

(Continued)

Table 1. (Continued)

Country	Unemployment Insurance[a]		Unemployment Assistance[a]		Unemployment Insurance Savings Accounts				Public Works[c]		Reference Variables	
	Replacement Rate (Percent of Individual's Pre-unemployment Wage where not Indicated Otherwise)	Maximum Duration (Months)	Replacement Rate	Maximum Duration (Months)	Replacement Rate (Percent of Individual's Pre-unemployment Wage)	Potential Duration	Contribution Rate (Employer + Worker Obligation)	Severance Pay[b] (Benefits After 20 Years of Service)	Participation Rates	Expenditure as Percent of GDP	Unemployment Rate[d]	Share of Informal Employment[e]
Ghana	n.a.	n.a.	n.a.	n.a.	n.a.	n.a.	n.a.	n.a.	0.1	—	—	72.3
Guinea	n.a.	n.a.	n.a.	n.a.	n.a.	n.a.	n.a.	n.a.	n.a.	n.a.	—	n.a.
Haiti	n.a.	n.a.	n.a.	n.a.	n.a.	n.a.	n.a.	n.a.	—	—	—	n.a.
Honduras	n.a.	n.a.	n.a.	n.a.	n.a.	n.a.	n.a.	8	1.8	—	3.7	—
India	n.a.	n.a.	n.a.	n.a.	n.a.	n.a.	n.a.	6	2.1	—	—	50.4
Indonesia	n.a.	n.a.	n.a.	n.a.	n.a.	n.a.	n.a.	9	2.2	—	5.2	37.4
Kenya	n.a.	n.a.	n.a.	n.a.	n.a.	n.a.	n.a.	10	0	—	—	40.8
Korea, Dem. People's Rep. of	n.a.	n.a.	n.a.	n.a.	n.a.	n.a.	n.a.	20	—	—	—	—
Kyrgyz Rep.	100%–150% of minimum wage	6	n.a.	n.a.	n.a.	n.a.	n.a.	1	—	—	—	40
Lao PDR	n.a.	n.a.	n.a.	n.a.	n.a.	n.a.	n.a.	n.a.	—	—	—	—
Liberia	n.a.	n.a.	n.a.	n.a.	n.a.	n.a.	n.a.	n.a.	n.a.	n.a.	—	—
Madagascar	n.a.	n.a.	n.a.	n.a.	n.a.	n.a.	n.a.	n.a.	—	n.a.	—	57.5
Malawi	n.a.	n.a.	n.a.	n.a.	n.a.	n.a.	n.a.	n.a.	—	n.a.	—	51.7
Mali	n.a.	n.a.	n.a.	n.a.	n.a.	n.a.	n.a.	n.a.	0.1	—	—	36
Mauritania	n.a.	n.a.	n.a.	n.a.	n.a.	n.a.	n.a.	n.a.	—	—	28.9	—
Moldova	50%–60% of average wage	—	n.a.	n.a.	n.a.	n.a.	n.a.	2	—	—	6.1	—
Mongolia	n.a.	n.a.	n.a.	n.a.	n.a.	n.a.	n.a.	1	—	—	5.7	11.5
Mozambique	n.a.	n.a.	n.a.	n.a.	n.a.	n.a.	n.a.	28.5	—	—	—	72.5
Myanmar	n.a.	n.a.	n.a.	n.a.	n.a.	n.a.	n.a.	n.a.	n.a.	n.a.	—	—

Table 1. (Continued)

Country	Unemployment Insurance[a] Replacement Rate (Percent of Individual's Pre-unemployment Wage where not Indicated Otherwise)	Unemployment Insurance[a] Maximum Duration (Months)	Unemployment Assistance[a] Replacement Rate	Unemployment Assistance[a] Maximum Duration (Months)	Unemployment Insurance Savings Accounts Replacement Rate (Percent of Individual's Pre-unemployment Wage)	Unemployment Insurance Savings Accounts Potential Duration	Unemployment Insurance Savings Accounts Contribution Rate (Employer + Worker Obligation)	Severance Pay[b] (Benefits After 20 Years of Service)	Public Works[c] Participation Rates	Public Works[c] Expenditure as Percent of GDP	Reference Variables Unemployment Rate[d]	Reference Variables Share of Informal Employment[e]
Nepal	n.a.	n.a.	n.a.	n.a.	n.a.	n.a.	n.a.	20	—	—	1.1	—
Nicaragua	n.a.	n.a.	n.a.	n.a.	n.a.	n.a.	n.a.	20	1.1	—	14.6	—
Niger	n.a.	n.a.	n.a.	n.a.	n.a.	n.a.	n.a.	6.8	0.2	—	—	—
Nigeria	n.a.	n.a.	n.a.	n.a.	n.a.	n.a.	n.a.	n.a.	—	—	7.8	48.9
Pakistan	n.a.	n.a.	n.a.	n.a.	n.a.	n.a.	n.a.	20	0.1	—	5.7	60
Rwanda	n.a.	n.a.	n.a.	n.a.	n.a.	n.a.	n.a.	n.a.	—	—	—	—
Senegal	n.a.	n.a.	n.a.	n.a.	n.a.	n.a.	n.a.	1	0.5	—	—	62.4
Sierra Leone	n.a.	n.a.	n.a.	n.a.	n.a.	n.a.	n.a.	n.a.	—	—	—	—
Somalia	n.a.	n.a.	n.a.	n.a.	n.a.	n.a.	n.a.	n.a.	n.a.	—	—	—
Sudan	n.a.	n.a.	n.a.	n.a.	n.a.	n.a.	n.a.	n.a.	—	—	—	—
Tajikistan	n.a.	n.a.	n.a.	n.a.	n.a.	n.a.	n.a.	n.a.	—	—	—	—
Tanzania, United Rep. of	n.a.	n.a.	n.a.	n.a.	n.a.	n.a.	n.a.	12	—	—	—	42.2
Togo	n.a.	n.a.	n.a.	n.a.	n.a.	n.a.	n.a.	n.a.	—	—	—	—
Turkmenistan	Limit of three monthly wages	n.a.	n.a.	n.a.	n.a.	n.a.	n.a.	n.a.	n.a.	n.a.	—	—
Uganda	n.a.	n.a.	n.a.	n.a.	n.a.	n.a.	n.a.	n.a.	—	—	7.4	56.4
Vietnam	n.a.	n.a.	n.a.	n.a.	n.a.	n.a.	n.a.	3	—	—	—	—
Yemen, Rep. of	n.a.	n.a.	n.a.	n.a.	n.a.	n.a.	n.a.	n.a.	—	—	11.5	—
Zambia	n.a.	n.a.	n.a.	n.a.	n.a.	n.a.	n.a.	n.a.	—	—	15	—
Zimbabwe	n.a.	n.a.	n.a.	n.a.	n.a.	n.a.	n.a.	n.a.	—	—	6.5	33.9

(Continued)

Table 1. (Continued)

Country	Unemployment Insurance[a] Replacement Rate (Percent of Individual's Pre-unemployment Wage where not Indicated Otherwise)	Unemployment Insurance[a] Maximum Duration (Months)	Unemployment Assistance[a] Replacement Rate	Unemployment Assistance[a] Maximum Duration (Months)	Unemployment Insurance Savings Accounts Replacement Rate (Percent of Individual's Pre-unemployment Wage)	Unemployment Insurance Savings Accounts Potential Duration	Unemployment Insurance Savings Accounts Contribution Rate (Employer + Worker Obligation)	Severance Pay[b] (Benefits After 20 Years of Service)	Public Works[c] Participation Rates	Public Works[c] Expenditure as Percent of GDP	Reference Variables Unemployment Rate[d]	Reference Variables Share of Informal Employment[e]
Lower-middle-income countries												
Albania	Flat	12–18	n.a.	n.a.	n.a.	n.a.	n.a.	10	—	—	15.8	—
Algeria	75%–300% of base	12–36	n.a.	n.a.	n.a.	n.a.	n.a.	n.a.	—	n.a.	28.3	—
Belarus	50%–70%	6.5	n.a.	n.a.	n.a.	n.a.	n.a.	3	—	—	2.7	—
Bolivia	n.a.	n.a.	n.a.	n.a.	n.a.	n.a.	n.a.	20	6.8	—	3.9	51.3
Bosnia and Herzegovina	30%–40%	3–12	n.a.	n.a.	n.a.	n.a.	n.a.	6.7	—	—	—	—
Bulgaria	60%	4–12	Flat	3	n.a.	n.a.	n.a.	1	—	0	14.8	63
Colombia	n.a.	n.a.	n.a.	n.a.	Lump sum	9.3% + 0	26.8	—	—	13.6	53.8	—
Costa Rica	n.a.	n.a.	n.a.	n.a.	n.a.	n.a.	n.a.	8	6.2	—	5.7	—
Cuba	n.a.	n.a.	n.a.	n.a.	n.a.	n.a.	n.a.	n.a.	n.a.	n.a.	—	—
Dominican Rep.	n.a.	n.a.	n.a.	n.a.	n.a.	n.a.	n.a.	15.3	n.a.	n.a.	16.1	52
Ecuador	n.a.	n.a.	n.a.	n.a.	Lump sum	8% + 0	20	—	—	12.8	58.8	—
Egypt, Arab Rep. of	60%	4–7	n.a.	n.a.	n.a.	n.a.	n.a.	n.a.	1.3	—	21.3	64.2
El Salvador	n.a.	n.a.	n.a.	n.a.	n.a.	n.a.	n.a.	n.a.	0.6	—	7.7	—
Georgia	Flat	6	n.a.	n.a.	n.a.	n.a.	n.a.	1	—	—	11.9	36.7
Guatemala	n.a.	n.a.	n.a.	n.a.	n.a.	n.a.	n.a.	20	—	—	—	—
Iran, Islamic Rep. of	55% of average wage	6–50	n.a.	n.a.	n.a.	n.a.	n.a.	20	n.a.	n.a.	—	—
Iraq	n.a.	n.a.	n.a.	n.a.	n.a.	n.a.	n.a.	n.a.	n.a.	n.a.	—	—

Table 1. (Continued)

Country	Unemployment Insurance[a] Replacement Rate (Percent of Individual's Pre-unemployment Wage where not Indicated Otherwise)	Unemployment Insurance[a] Maximum Duration (Months)	Unemployment Assistance[a] Replacement Rate	Unemployment Assistance[a] Maximum Duration (Months)	Unemployment Insurance Savings Accounts Replacement Rate (Percent of Individual's Pre-unemployment Wage)	Unemployment Insurance Savings Accounts Potential Duration	Unemployment Insurance Savings Accounts Contribution Rate (Employer + Worker Obligation)	Severance Pay[b] (Benefits After 20 Years of Service)	Public Works[c] Participation Rates	Public Works[c] Expenditure as Percent of GDP	Reference Variables Unemployment Rate[d]	Reference Variables Share of Informal Employment[e]
Jamaica	n.a.	n.a.	n.a.	n.a.	n.a.	n.a.	n.a.	n.a.	—	—	16	—
Jordan	n.a.	n.a.	n.a.	n.a.	n.a.	n.a.	n.a.	20	n.a.	n.a.	15	—
Kazakhstan	n.a.	n.a.	n.a.	n.a.	n.a.	n.a.	n.a.	1	n.a.	n.a.	12.7	40
Latvia	90%	6	n.a.	n.a.	n.a.	n.a.	n.a.	1	—	—	16	—
Lithuania	50%	6	n.a.	n.a.	n.a.	n.a.	n.a.	24	—	—	15	—
Macedonia, FYR	40%–50%	24	n.a.	n.a.	n.a.	n.a.	n.a.	10	—	—	33.4	—
Morocco	n.a.	n.a.	n.a.	n.a.	n.a.	n.a.	n.a.	n.a.	—	—	19.8	—
Papua New Guinea	n.a.	n.a.	n.a.	n.a.	n.a.	n.a.	n.a.	n.a.	n.a.	n.a.	—	—
Paraguay	n.a.	n.a.	n.a.	n.a.	n.a.	n.a.	n.a.	n.a.	n.a.	n.a.	8.2	—
Peru	n.a.	n.a.	n.a.	n.a.	Lump sum	8% + 0	12	0.8	0	7.6	54.6	—
Philippines	n.a.	n.a.	n.a.	n.a.	n.a.	n.a.	n.a.	20	0	—	8.6	30.6
Romania	50%–55%	9	30%	18	n.a.	n.a.	n.a.	n.a.	—	—	6.8	42.7
Russian Federation	45%–75%	n.a.	n.a.	n.a.	n.a.	n.a.	n.a.	1	—	—	11.5	42.2
South Africa	45%	6	n.a.	n.a.	n.a.	n.a.	n.a.	5	—	—	21.2	—
Sri Lanka	n.a.	n.a.	n.a.	n.a.	n.a.	n.a.	n.a.	20	—	—	11.3	31.3
Swaziland	n.a.	n.a.	n.a.	n.a.	n.a.	n.a.	n.a.	n.a.	n.a.	n.a.	—	—

(Continued)

Table 1. (Continued)

Country	Unemployment Insurance[a] Replacement Rate (Percent of Individual's Pre-unemployment Wage where not Indicated Otherwise)	Unemployment Insurance[a] Maximum Duration (Months)	Unemployment Assistance[a] Replacement Rate	Unemployment Assistance[a] Maximum Duration (Months)	Unemployment Insurance Savings Accounts Replacement Rate (Percent of Individual's Pre-unemployment Wage)	Unemployment Insurance Savings Accounts Potential Duration	Unemployment Insurance Savings Accounts Contribution Rate (Employer + Worker Obligation)	Severance Pay[b] (Benefits After 20 Years of Service)	Public Works[c] Participation Rates	Public Works[c] Expenditure as Percent of GDP	Reference Variables Unemployment Rate[d]	Reference Variables Share of Informal Employment[e]
Syrian Arab Rep.	n.a.	n.a.	n.a.	n.a.	n.a.	n.a.	n.a.	17.5	n.a.	n.a.	—	—
Thailand	n.a.	n.a.	n.a.	n.a.	n.a.	n.a.	n.a.	10	—	—	1.9	—
Tunisia	n.a.	n.a.	Minimum wage	3	n.a.	n.a.	n.a.	3	n.a.	n.a.	—	57.1
Ukraine	35%–60%	12	75% of minimum wage	6	n.a.	n.a.	n.a.	1	—	—	9.1	—
Uzbekistan	50%	6	n.a.	n.a.	n.a.	n.a.	n.a.	2	—	—	**0.4**	—
Yugoslavia, Fed. Rep. (Serbia/Montenegro)	n.a.	n.a.	70%	3–30	n.a.	n.a.	n.a.	4	—	—	—	—
Upper-middle-income countries												
Argentina	60%	4–12	n.a.	n.a.	Lump sum (available only in construction)	12% (8% after first year) + 0	10	6.4	—	15.9	—	—
Botswana	n.a.	n.a.	n.a.	n.a.	n.a.	n.a.	n.a.	3	10.2	—	21.5	—
Brazil	50%	6–11	n.a.	n.a.	Lump sum, plus 40% of individual's pre-unemployment wage if not dismissed for "just cause"	8% + 0	6	—	—	7.9	49.2	—

Table 1. (Continued)

Country	Unemployment Insurance[a] Replacement Rate (Percent of Individual's Pre-unemployment Wage where not Indicated Otherwise)	Maximum Duration (Months)	Unemployment Assistance[a] Replacement Rate	Maximum Duration (Months)	Unemployment Insurance Savings Accounts Replacement Rate (Percent of Individual's Pre-unemployment Wage)	Potential Duration	Contribution Rate (Employer + Worker Obligation)	Severance Pay[b] (Benefits After 20 Years of Service)	Public Works[c] Participation Rates	Expenditure as Percent of GDP	Unemployment Rate[d]	Share of Informal Employment[e]
Chile	n.a.	n.a.	n.a.	n.a.	30–50%	5 months	2.4% + 0.6%	11	7.7	—	6.5	40
Croatia	60%–80%	2.5–10	16% of average wage (in 2001)	—	n.a.	n.a.	n.a.	10	—	—	11.2	70
Czech Republic	40%–50%	6	n.a.	n.a.	n.a.	n.a.	n.a.	2	0.2	0	5.6	—
Estonia	n.a.	n.a.	$23	6	n.a.	n.a.	n.a.	4	—	0	10.2	—
Gabon	n.a.	n.a.	n.a.	n.a.	n.a.	n.a.	n.a.	—	n.a.	n.a.	—	—
Hungary	65%	9–12	Flat	9	n.a.	n.a.	n.a.	5	2.2	0.2	8.7	—
Korea, Rep. of	50%	3–8	n.a.	n.a.	n.a.	n.a.	n.a.	20	5.2	—	3.9	—
Lebanon	n.a.	n.a.	n.a.	n.a.	n.a.	n.a.	n.a.	10	—	—	**8.6**	—
Libya	n.a.	n.a.	n.a.	n.a.	n.a.	n.a.	n.a.	—	n.a.	n.a.	—	—
Malaysia	n.a.	n.a.	n.a.	n.a.	n.a.	n.a.	n.a.	12	—	—	2.9	—
Mauritius	n.a.	n.a.	n.a.	n.a.	n.a.	n.a.	n.a.	n.a.	—	—	**9.8**	—
Mexico	n.a.	n.a.	n.a.	n.a.	n.a.	n.a.	n.a.	17.4	4.4	0.5	3.7	—
Oman	n.a.	n.a.	n.a.	n.a.	n.a.	n.a.	n.a.	n.a.	n.a.	n.a.	—	—
Panama	n.a.	n.a.	n.a.	n.a.	Lump sum	—	5	0.7	—	13.4	—	—
Poland	Flat, 23% of average wage (in 2001)	6–18	n.a.	n.a.	n.a.	n.a.	n.a.	n.a.	0.7	0.1	12	—
Saudi Arabia	n.a.	n.a.	n.a.	n.a.	n.a.	n.a.	n.a.	17.5	n.a.	n.a.	—	—

(Continued)

Table 1. (Continued)

Country	Unemployment Insurance[a] Replacement Rate (Percent of Individual's Pre-unemployment Wage where not Indicated Otherwise)	Unemployment Insurance[a] Maximum Duration (Months)	Unemployment Assistance[a] Replacement Rate	Unemployment Assistance[a] Maximum Duration (Months)	Unemployment Insurance Savings Accounts Replacement Rate (Percent of Individual's Pre-unemployment Wage)	Unemployment Insurance Savings Accounts Potential Duration	Unemployment Insurance Savings Accounts Contribution Rate (Employer + Worker Obligation)	Severance Pay[b] (Benefits After 20 Years of Service)	Public Works[c] Participation Rates	Public Works[c] Expenditure as Percent of GDP	Reference Variables Unemployment Rate[d]	Reference Variables Share of Informal Employment[e]
Slovak Rep.	45%–50%	6–9	Flat	6	n.a.	n.a.	n.a.	2	—	0	13	—
Trinidad and Tobago	n.a.	n.a.	n.a.	n.a.	n.a.	n.a.	n.a.	n.a.	n.a.	n.a.	15.1	—
Turkey	50%	6–10	n.a.	n.a.	n.a.	n.a.	n.a.	20	—	—	6.9	—
Uruguay	n.a.	n.a.	n.a.	n.a.	50%	6 months	15% + 12.5% (comprehensive insurance)	6	n.a.	n.a.	10.5	—
Venezuela, R.B. de	60%	3–6	n.a.	n.a.	Lump sum	—	9	n.a.	n.a.	11.9	—	
High-income countries												
Australia	n.a.	n.a.	41%–99% of average wage (in 2001)	No limit	n.a.	n.a.	n.a.	2	0.3	0.1	7.9	6.4
Austria	55% of net earnings	5–18	51% of net earnings	6 (extendable)	Lump sum	1.53	9	—	0	4.9	16	
Belgium	44%–60%	No limit	n.a.	n.a.	n.a.	n.a.	n.a.	n.a.	3.2	0.5	9.1	—
Canada	55%	11	n.a.	n.a.	n.a.	n.a.	n.a.	1.3	0.1	0.1	8.8	4.4
Denmark	90%	12–48	n.a.	n.a.	n.a.	n.a.	n.a.	3	0.8	0.2	5.9	15.4
Finland	Up to 90%	16.5	Flat	No limit	n.a.	n.a.	n.a.	1	2	0.3	12.9	—
France	57%–75%	4–60	—	No limit	n.a.	n.a.	n.a.	2	1.5	0.2	11.9	9

Table 1. (Continued)

Country	Unemployment Insurance[a] Replacement Rate (Percent of Individual's Pre-unemployment Wage where not Indicated Otherwise)	Unemployment Insurance[a] Maximum Duration (Months)	Unemployment Assistance[a] Replacement Rate	Unemployment Assistance[a] Maximum Duration (Months)	Unemployment Insurance Savings Accounts Replacement Rate (Percent of Individual's Pre-unemployment Wage)	Unemployment Insurance Savings Accounts Potential Duration	Unemployment Insurance Savings Accounts Contribution Rate (Employer + Worker Obligation)	Severance Pay[b] (Benefits After 20 Years of Service)	Public Works[c] Participation Rates	Public Works[c] Expenditure as Percent of GDP	Reference Variables Unemployment Rate[d]	Reference Variables Share of Informal Employment[e]
Germany	60% of net earnings	6–32	53% of net earnings	No limit	n.a.	n.a.	n.a.	n.a.	1.6	0.3	9	22
Greece	40%–50%	4–9	n.a.	n.a.	n.a.	n.a.	n.a.	5.8	n.a.	n.a.	9.8	—
Hong Kong, China	n.a.	n.a.	$165–$231 per month (2002)	No limit	n.a.	n.a.	n.a.	2	n.a.	n.a.	3.8	—
Ireland	Flat, 13% of average wage (in 2001)	15	Flat, 13% of average wage (in 2001)	No limit	n.a.	n.a.	n.a.	2.5	3.7	0.6	9.6	—
Israel	40%–80% of average wage	4.5/year	n.a.	n.a.	n.a.	n.a.	n.a.	20	—	n.a.	7.7	—
Italy	40%–80%	6–27	n.a.	n.a.	n.a.	n.a.	n.a.	18	—	0	11.5	39
Japan	60%–80%	10	n.a.	n.a.	n.a.	n.a.	n.a.	20	n.a.	n.a.	3.8	—
Kuwait	$250–$680 (in 2002)	12	n.a.	n.a.	n.a.	n.a.	n.a.	n.a.	n.a.	n.a.	—	—
Netherlands	70%	6–60	Flat, 70% of minimum wage	24	n.a.	n.a.	n.a.	n.a.	0.3	0.4	5.4	—

(Continued)

Table 1. (Continued)

Country	Unemployment Insurance[a] Replacement Rate (Percent of Individual's Pre-unemployment Wage where not Indicated Otherwise)	Unemployment Insurance[a] Maximum Duration (Months)	Unemployment Assistance[a] Replacement Rate	Unemployment Assistance[a] Maximum Duration (Months)	Unemployment Insurance Savings Accounts Replacement Rate (Percent of Individual's Pre-unemployment Wage)	Unemployment Insurance Savings Accounts Potential Duration	Unemployment Insurance Savings Accounts Contribution Rate (Employer + Worker Obligation)	Severance Pay[b] (Benefits After 20 Years of Service)	Public Works[c] Participation Rates	Public Works[c] Expenditure as Percent of GDP	Reference Variables Unemployment Rate[d]	Reference Variables Share of Informal Employment[e]
New Zealand	n.a.	n.a.	15%–40% of average wage (in 2001)	No limit	n.a.	n.a.	n.a.	11	0.9	0	6.7	—
Norway	73%	18–36	n.a.	n.a.	n.a.	n.a.	n.a.	n.a.	0.1	0	4	—
Portugal	65%	12–30	Flat, 80% of minimum wage	12–30	n.a.	n.a.	n.a.	20	0.8	0.1	6.2	—
Singapore	n.a.	n.a.			n.a.	n.a.	n.a.	20	n.a.	n.a.	3.2	—
Slovenia	60%–70%	3–24	Flat, 80% of minimum wage	15	n.a.	n.a.	n.a.	10	1.1	0.1	7.4	31
Spain	60%–70%	24	Flat	6–18	n.a.	n.a.	n.a.	12	1.4	0.1	20	21.9
Sweden	75%	10	Flat	5	n.a.	n.a.	n.a.	n.a.	2.7	0.4	8.8	19.8
Switzerland	70%	5–17	n.a.	n.a.	n.a.	n.a.	n.a.	n.a.	0	0.2	3.4	—
Taiwan, China	60%	6	n.a.	n.a.	n.a.	n.a.	n.a.	7	n.a.	n.a.	2.8	—

Table 1. (Continued)

Country	Unemployment Insurance[a] Replacement Rate (Percent of Individual's Pre-unemployment Wage where not Indicated Otherwise)	Maximum Duration (Months)	Unemployment Assistance[a] Replacement Rate	Maximum Duration (Months)	Unemployment Insurance Savings Accounts Replacement Rate (Percent of Individual's Pre-unemployment Wage)	Potential Duration	Contribution Rate (Employer + Worker Obligation)	Severance Pay[b] (Benefits After 20 Years of Service)	Public Works[c] Participation Rates	Expenditure as Percent of GDP	Reference Variables Unemployment Rate[d]	Share of Informal Employment[e]
United Kingdom	Flat, 41% of average wage (in 2001)	6	Flat	No limit	n.a.	n.a.	n.a.	5	0.1	—	6.5	—
United States	50%	6.5–10	n.a.	n.a.	n.a.	n.a.	n.a.	n.a.	0.1	0	5	—

—, not available; n.a., not applicable.

Note: Included are countries covered in U.S. Social Security Administration (1999) with populations of 1 million or more.

[a]Reference period for countries in Europe and East Asia and the Pacific is 2002; for all other countries reference period is 1999. Replacement rates are percentage of gross wages, unless specified otherwise. Benefit levels in dollars are benefits in local currency converted into dollars at average yearly exchange rates. For Algeria base is average monthly salary plus monthly national guaranteed minimum salary divided

[b]Reference period is 1999. Benefits refer to months of salary paid to dismissed employee with 20 years of service. Figure for Sri Lanka is an estimate (box 1).

[c]For developing and transition countries, includes social funds. Reference period is the 1990s and 2000–02 (yearly average or single year). Participation rate is defined as 100 times the number of participants divided by the labor force.

[d]Five-year averages for 1995–99 (if single year, numbers appear in boldface and refer to one of the years during 1995–2000).

[e]Estimates of the share of the labor force employed in the unofficial economy in the capital city as a percent of the official labor. Reference period is late 1990s. Figures are based on surveys and, for some countries, econometric estimates.

Source: Unemployment insurance, unemployment assistance: U.S. Social Security Administration (1999, 2002a, 2002b); OECD (1999); Vodopivec, Wörgötter, and Raju (2005). Unemployment insurance savings accounts: Koman, Schuh, and Weber (forthcoming); Acevedo, Eskenazi, and Pages (forthcoming); Heckman and Pages (2000); Lipsett (1999); Mazza (1999). Severance payments: Botero and others (2002); OECD (1999). Public works: World Bank databases on public works and social funds projects, available at www1.worldbank.org/sp/safetynets; Betcherman and Islam (2001); Beegle, Frankenberg, and Thomas (1999); Marquez (1999); Subbarao (1997, 2003). Unemployment: ILO (2001); World Bank (2003). Share of informal employment: Botero and others (2002).

It should be emphasized that social insurance, including unemployment insurance, is a response of modern industrial society to the changing nature of the labor market, above all to the development of a modern employment relationship (Atkinson 1995a). In an industrialized and urbanized society, employment becomes discretionary: workers either work or do not work. This development has strong implications for unemployment—if they cannot find a job in wage employment (working for others), workers are unable to resort to self- or home-production, because they are divorced from ownership of the means of production. Similarly, in industrial societies, older and less productive workers stop working altogether once their productivity drops substantially. In contrast, in traditional societies they continue to be economically active as long as they produce something of value. The "invention" of unemployment and the changing nature of retirement created the need to insure against non-employment contingencies. Social insurance is thus based on the concepts of unemployment and retirement as specific social constructs.

Unemployment insurance has four key strengths.[1] First, because it pools resources across a wide base, it provides good protection (that is, enables strong consumption smoothing) for all covered workers. Studies on the United States find that the average welfare of benefit recipient households is only 3–8 percent lower than that of households whose head is employed (Hamermesh and Slesnick 1995); in the absence of unemployment insurance, average consumption expenditures would fall about 20 percent (Gruber 1997). Second, the system performs well under all types of shocks. During the 1990s, when transition countries experienced massive increases in unemployment, the system provided effective insurance against idiosyncratic, sectoral, regional, and, somewhat less successfully, national shocks (there was some scaling back of benefits when unemployment escalated economywide; see Vodopivec, Wörgötter, and Raju 2005). Third, by automatically injecting additional resources and reducing taxes during recessions, unemployment insurance acts as an automatic stabilizer and thus moderates the magnitude of the economic downturn. Empirical evidence for Canada and the United States shows that unemployment insurance reduces GDP losses during downturns by 10–15 percent (Dungan and Murphy 1995; Chimerine, Black, and Coffey 1999; Hamermesh 1992). Fourth, unemployment insurance encourages the emergence or expansion of more risky jobs and industries, which may increase efficiency (Acemoglu and Shimer 1999, 2000).

These strengths have to be weighed against four weaknesses. First, the system creates reemployment disincentives and wage pressures, which increase the equilibrium unemployment rate of the economy (see, for example, Holmlund 1998).[2] Second, by interacting with adverse shocks, the system contributes to the persistence of unemployment (Blanchard and Wolfers 2000). Third, unemployment insurance may create large unfunded liabilities, which put pressure on the government to subsidize the system.[3] Fourth, protection is limited to formal sector workers.

Unemployment Assistance

Unemployment assistance is a means-tested form of income support granted to working-age individuals who are unemployed and lack the necessary financial resources to maintain a minimum standard of living for themselves and their families. Self-standing unemployment assistance exists in few countries, notably Australia; Hong Kong, China; and New Zealand, among high-income countries, and Tunisia and Serbia and Montenegro among middle-income countries (table 1). In all other countries in which it is offered, unemployment assistance exists in tandem with unemployment insurance and is available upon expiration of eligibility to unemployment insurance to those unemployed who pass the means test.

Like unemployment insurance, unemployment assistance systems require applicants to be capable of, looking for, and available for work. In some countries, eligibility for unemployment assistance is not conditional on previous employment or contribution history. However, in most countries, particularly those with dual unemployment insurance/assistance systems, unemployment assistance is an extension of the unemployment insurance offered to the long-term unemployed who have satisfied some minimum length of employment and do not have the economic means to support their households. Means- or income-testing is conducted not only on the financial resources of the applicant but also on that of the applicant's spouse and other adult members within the household. The system is typically financed by governments through general tax revenues. In countries with dual unemployment insurance/assistance systems, the source of financing is usually the same as for unemployment insurance.

Unlike unemployment insurance, which grants benefits to all workers with sufficient paid contributions, unemployment assistance screens potential benefit recipients with an income/means test. This feature generates outcomes that are different from those of unemployment insurance in terms of both income protection and efficiency.

Unemployment assistance has two main advantages over unemployment insurance. First, it is better able than unemployment insurance system to redistribute income to the poor (although, interestingly, it does not necessarily generate savings, as shown below). Second, the system can offer benefits to workers with weak labor force attachment, including informal sector workers, who are typically outside the reach of unemployment insurance.

Unemployment assistance also has six disadvantages compared with unemployment insurance. First, it offers lower level of protection to high-income workers. Second, it imposes larger administrative costs (the costs of monitoring income and assets of initial and ongoing claims). Third, it may reduce the system's take-up. As Atkinson (1995b) shows, in Western countries a third or more of potential claimants never receive means-tested benefits (because of information problems, administrative complexities, and stigmatization of recipients). Fourth, because unemployment assistance benefits are contingent on the household income (and assets) of the unemployed individual, they may reduce the labor supply of other family members (for evidence from transition countries, see Vodopivec, Wörgötter, and Raju 2005). Fifth, unemployment assistance may create perverse entitlement effects. Young people may claim to be unemployed in order to collect benefits, for example, even though they may not be seriously searching for work or engaged in training. Sixth, unemployment assistance may discourage savings, because capital enters the income and asset tests (Atkinson and Micklewright 1991).

Unemployment Insurance Savings Accounts

Unemployment insurance savings accounts are a relatively new instrument, used only in Latin America and Austria (table 1). The accounts try to weave self-insurance into social insurance. Employers and workers deposit contributions into the savings accounts of individual workers; upon becoming unemployed, workers finance their unemployment benefits by withdrawing from these accounts. Upon retirement, positive account balances are added to workers' pensions. Under some proposals, unemployed workers are able to draw benefits under rules similar to traditional unemployment insurance, switching to funding from the solidarity fund when they exhaust resources in their individual accounts (the solidarity fund is financed by contributions from workers and employers and may be subsidized by the government; access to the fund is limited).

The most important advantage of the system is arguably the reduction in the moral hazard inherent in traditional unemployment insurance, because the system internalizes the costs of unemployment benefits.[4] Because the benefit is payable in cases of voluntary separations, the system encourages labor reallocation and cuts down on the litigation costs incurred under severance pay. If backed by government subsidies, the system has the potential of attracting informal sector workers.

These strengths have to be weighed against four shortcomings. First, the system—in its pure form—does not pool risk among individuals and may thus be less efficient than social insurance systems. (For example, young workers may not be able to accumulate enough savings at the time of separation to be able to self-finance their unemployment.) Second, the version of the system that allows individuals to borrow from their accounts may suffer from a moral hazard problem of its own: it may generate incentives to withdraw from the formal sector and find a job in the informal sector, thereby avoiding the repayment of the debt upon reemployment in the formal sector (Parsons forthcoming). Third, the system requires a relatively well-functioning financial sector. Fourth, the system has higher administrative costs than other systems.

Severance Pay

Severance pay, typically either mandated or required by collective agreements, provides a lump-sum benefit to qualifying laid-off workers. Its coverage in developing countries is often limited to sectors, industries, or firms above a certain size. MacIsaac and Rama (2000) estimate that only about 20 percent of private sector workers, most of them wealthier workers, are legally entitled to severance pay in Peru. Benefits usually depend on years of service and individual's earnings. They are paid by employers, sometimes with government assistance (for a review of the origin, economic rationale, and current attempts to reform severance pay systems around the world, see Holzmann, Iyer, and Vodopivec forthcoming). Except in low-income countries, severance pay is the most prevalent income support system in developing countries.

Because it often offers inadequate income protection and may impose large efficiency costs, severance pay is often considered one of the least appropriate options of income support. It does have three strengths, however. First, because the amount of severance pay is not contingent on the duration of subsequent unemployment, the system minimizes disincentives for subsequent job search. Second, by offering risk-pooling at the level of the firm, it may, if the scheme is generous enough, offer solid income protection. Third, administration of the system is simple.

Severance pay suffers from several weaknesses, related to both income protection and efficiency. On the income protection front, there are two main weaknesses. First, the system suffers from the so-called "nonperformance problem" (the fact that despite legal entitlement, many workers fail to obtain benefits). MacIsaac and Rama (2000) estimate that only about half of all workers legally entitled to severance pay are likely to receive the benefit if dismissed (the payment is more likely if workers have a written contract and if they work in a larger, unionized firm that pays social security contributions). In Malaysia, employers disbursed only 83 percent of the severance pay claims of workers laid off in 1998 (Mansor and others 2001). Nonperformance is related to the limited risk-pooling ability of the system, coupled with the nonfunded nature of the system and the fact that the liabilities often arise when the firm is least capable of paying them. Second, severance pay benefits are inefficient, as the same amount is paid regardless of the duration of the unemployment spell. MacIssac and Rama (2000) find that severance pay was overly generous in Peru, where per capita consumption of those unemployed who received severance pay was higher than the consumption of otherwise similar workers who were employed.

On the efficiency front, severance pay's scorecard is also rather negative. First, several studies show that strict employment protection reduces employment. Lazear (1990) finds that severance pay reduces both employment and labor force participation. Fallon and Lucas (1991) show that strengthening job security regulations led to a strong decline in employment in India and Zimbabwe. More recent studies confirming the link between job security and lower employment include Haffner and others (2001) for Organization for Economic Cooperation and Development (OECD) countries, Heckman and Pages (2000) for OECD and Latin-American countries, Besley and Burgess (2004) for India, and Haltiwanger, Scarpetta, and Vodopivec (2003) for OECD and transition countries. Heckman and Pages (2000) attribute a reduction in employment of 5 percentage points to job security provisions in Latin America. OECD (1999) finds insignificant effects on overall employment rates but notes that negative effects are concentrated among prime-age women, young people, and older workers. Studies also show that severance pay increases part-time employment and self-employment.

Second, mounting evidence suggests that severance pay reduces inflows to and outflows from unemployment. By doing so, it contributes to longer unemployment spells; flows through employment may not be affected as strongly (for a recent survey, see OECD 1999; for evidence on transition countries, see Haltiwanger, Scarpetta, and Vodopivec 2003). Reduced labor market flows may hinder labor force adjustment and the reallocation of jobs, thereby slowing aggregate productivity growth (for a survey of the effects of job reallocation on aggregate productivity growth, see Davis and Haltiwanger 1999). Third, de Ferranti and others (2000) report large litigation costs arising from disputes over the cause of separation in Latin America.

Public Works

Among systems that do not, strictly speaking, provide insurance, public works are worth singling out. Public works provide publicly financed, low-wage work to poor people. These programs are geared toward labor-intensive projects, with wages often set below the prevailing market rate. Public works have multiple objectives, with income support and the provision of goods and services the most important ones. In low-income countries, public works are the most prevalent income support program, available in more than 80 percent of countries. Interestingly, the incidence of public works is also relatively high in middle- and high-income countries (table 1).

Public works programs have several strengths. They are effective in reaching the poor, have good targeting properties, and have substantial capacity to redistribute income from the rich to the poor. These programs also have strong capacity to attract informal sector workers, and they allow flexible and rapid responses to shocks (Subbarao 2003). Moreover, public works are administratively less demanding than other public income support systems for the unemployed.

There are also four weaknesses of the program. First, high nonwage costs reduce the effectiveness of public works in reaching the poor. Ravallion (1999) estimates that $5 of public transfers are needed to increase the earnings of the poor by $1, partly because of the leakage of spending on the nonpoor. Second, the countercyclical pattern of funding shows that it is difficult to raise funding during crises, when support is needed most (Wodon 2000). Third, because of highly redistributive character of public works, it may be difficult to gain political support; some leakage to the nonpoor may be necessary to gain such support. Ravallion (1991), for example, finds that the leakage of benefits to nonpoor participants in the Maharashtra Employment Guarantee Scheme in India may have been instrumental in obtaining sustained budgetary support. Fourth, public works may stigmatize participants (for the experience in transition countries, see Betcherman, Olivas, and Dar 2004).

Distributional Effects of Income Support Systems

Different income support systems have different effects on income redistribution. Vodopivec (2004) shows that among the income support systems discussed here, public works are the most progressive. Subbarao (2003) also documents the strong potential of public works for redistribution. He reports that nearly 100 percent of public works participants in Chile and 60–70 percent in India (both in the nationwide program and the Maharashtra Employment Guarantee Scheme) were poor. Based on their analysis of 101 national public works projects in South Africa, Haddad and Adato (2001) conclude that under fairly robust assumptions, the vast majority of public works programs considerably outperform hypothetical benchmarks consisting of untargeted transfers. This does not mean that the targeting method under public works—self-selection based on working in the program—outperforms other social safety net programs that use different targeting methods. After comparing the effectiveness of various targeting methods in 67 programs, Coady, Grosch, and Hoddinott (2004) conclude that no method provides clear advantages.[5] Although a public works program (Argentina's Trabajar) received the highest score for its targeting performance, three public works programs ranked among the worst 10 programs. Coady, Grosch, and Hoddinott also find considerable evidence that it is the implementation of the program, rather than the method of targeting, that is key to successful targeting.[6]

Unemployment assistance also has a strong redistributive potential. In a study of 13 OECD countries, Vroman (2002) shows that the share of unemployment benefits received by the bottom three deciles ranged from 20.8 percent in Italy to 58.0 percent in Australia, the only country in the study with a self-standing unemployment assistance system. The top three deciles in Australia received 7.4 percent of transfers, the lowest percentage across the 13 countries.

The income distribution effects of unemployment insurance and unemployment assistance in transition countries are also strongly progressive. Vodopivec,

Wörgötter, and Raju (2005) show that in the mid-1990s, the bottom 40 percent of households in seven European transition countries received 70–80 percent of the benefits. They report that when considering distributions of households with at least one unemployed member, the incidence of benefits was progressive when distribution was based on pre-benefit income and regressive when based on post-benefit income. The exceptions are Estonia and the Slovak Republic, the countries with the smallest share of unemployment benefits in household incomes, where the small scale of transfers did not make a difference in the post-benefit distribution.

The strong redistributive performance of unemployment benefits in transition countries may be the result of circumstances—such as nearly universal unemployment benefit coverage—that are not present in developing countries. Brazil's unemployment benefit system has a neutral effect on the redistribution of income (de Ferranti and others 2000). Unemployment benefits have not been an important tool for income redistribution in industrial countries: unemployment benefits are progressive in about half of OECD countries and neutral in the other half (Forster 2000). Nonetheless, the evidence on transition countries suggests that under specific circumstances, unemployment insurance and assistance systems offer substantial scope for income redistribution.

De Ferranti and others (2000) show that most participants in both the Colombian unemployment insurance savings accounts and the Peruvian severance pay system belong to the richest segments of the population (this pattern is not an inherent property of these systems, but it is probably typical for low-income countries). In addition to affecting income distribution directly, severance pay also has an indirect effect, by hindering access to jobs by disadvantaged groups. Blanchard (2000) shows that an increase in firing costs leads to higher unemployment of marginal groups of workers because of their inferior access to jobs. Because the productivity of these workers before hiring is not easily revealed, their probability of being hired in the presence of increased firing costs is lower. Indeed, an OECD study (1999) finds that stricter employment protection legislation reduces employment among prime-age women and young people, rendering them more susceptible to unemployment risk. By contributing to labor market dualism, severance pay thus increases the advantage of already privileged formal sector workers, increasing inequalities in society. In line with these findings, Besley and Burgess (2004) show that "pro-worker" legislation may work against the poor in developing countries.

What are the likely distributive effects of introducing unemployment insurance savings accounts? While in principle the system can provide the same income protection as traditional unemployment insurance system, switching from unemployment insurance to unemployment insurance savings accounts changes income distribution because the benefits are financed differently.

Simulations suggest that the distributive effects for the United States are likely to be small and regressive. Feldstein and Altman (1998) find that individuals in all quintiles gain slightly and individuals in the bottom quintile lose slightly (the fact that these estimates do not take account of the behavioral responses to the changed system most likely means that they understate the distributive effects). Similar simulations for Estonia show that the income redistribution achieved by unemployment insurance savings accounts is substantially less than that achieved under unemployment insurance and that unemployment insurance savings accounts allow for more redistribution when unemployment is higher and unemployment benefits more generous (Vodopivec and Rejec forthcoming).

Choosing a System

In choosing among income support systems for the unemployed, policymakers should base their decisions on the strengths and weaknesses of the systems as well as on country-specific circumstances. Depending on institutional capacity and the development of the labor market, some countries may find social insurance an attractive option. Other countries may try to improve their severance pay systems, including by converting them into unemployment accounts. To provide protection to informal sector workers, policymakers should also consider public works and innovative approaches.

This section discusses how alternative income support systems fit institutional and other circumstances typically found in developing and transition countries. It draws policy implications about choosing among them (see Vodopivec 2004).

What Conditions Are Conducive for Unemployment Insurance?

Several institutional and labor market features are conducive for unemployment insurance. The first is strong administrative capacity to monitor initial and particularly continuing eligibility. Recent studies suggest that effective monitoring and the use of sanctions can strongly reduce the average duration of unemployment benefit payments and increase the transition rate to employment (OECD 2000; Boone and others 2001. Thus the stricter the monitoring of the behavior of recipients, the milder the disincentives of unemployment insurance.

A second feature is an informal sector that is not too large. The higher the informality of the economy, the more abundant are opportunities for undeclared paid work and thus the higher the costs of monitoring.

A third feature is the low incidence of private transfers. If the introduction of public insurance breaks down the habit of self-help among extended families in communities, replacing private transfers by social insurance may be welfare reducing (Attanasio and Rios-Rull 2000).

Absent these conditions, unemployment insurance does not perform well, increasing inefficiencies, reducing welfare gains, or both. For example, reemployment incentives depend crucially on a country's monitoring capacity. This capacity determines how strictly the conditions of initial and, perhaps even more important, continuing eligibility are imposed. As the experience with Argentinean unemployment insurance suggests, the capacity to screen initial eligibility has not been a problem—the system draws on the capacity of other social protection systems—but the country still has to monitor continuing eligibility (Mazza 1999). Inadequate monitoring creates leakages that add to the costs of the system.

In view of the above, how suitable is unemployment insurance in developing countries? Prompted by increased exposure to foreign markets and fearing future international crises, some developing countries (including the Philippines and Sri Lanka) are contemplating introducing unemployment insurance. Immediate introduction in a country like the Philippines may be premature before certain conditions are fulfilled (Yoo 2001). Gill and Ilahi (2000) argue that many Latin-American countries lack the capacity to run an efficient unemployment insurance system. They argue that although introducing unemployment insurance should be a long-term goal of these countries, it is either infeasible or too costly a strategy in the medium term. They propose that Latin-American governments augment other instruments, such as self-insurance, to overcome the lack of market insurance in the medium term.

In sum, because successful performance of unemployment insurance relies on strong administrative capacity to monitor system eligibility and an informal sector that is not too large—conditions typically lacking in developing and transition countries—the case for its introduction in these countries is less compelling than it is in developed countries. The presence of unemployment insurance may also reduce incentives for self-protection and break down the habit of self-help within communities. Introducing full-scale, general unemployment insurance is thus viewed as a longer-term goal for most developing countries. Under suitable circumstances, countries with the most pressing needs could consider introducing a scheme with modest benefits and limited coverage (a scheme offered by larger employers, for example). Of course, to ensure affordability, minimize adverse effects, and enable a smooth start, a new unemployment insurance system has to provide modest benefits and be introduced on a small scale. Moreover, it can be introduced only after the needed support infrastructure is put in place. Specific historic and political conditions may be instrumental in introducing such a system (box 1).

Box 1. Improving Income Support for the Unemployed in Sri Lanka

By reforming its nontransparent, discretionary, and costly severance pay program, Sri Lanka could improve income protection of the unemployed while promoting employment and efficient reallocation of labor and ensuring more equitable access to formal sector jobs. The current severance pay system not only provides extremely high compensation to laid-off workers—and imposes correspondingly high costs on employers— its discretionary nature and lack of transparency impose additional costs by creating lengthy procedures and generating uncertainty about firms' ability to lay off workers. Consequences of high separation costs include lower labor market flows, reduced aggregate employment, and repressed investment incentives, especially for foreign investors.

Currently, the government sets the amount of compensation to laid-off workers and has the authority to reject employers' demands. In 2000–01 the average compensation amounted to two to three monthly wages per year of service, and total payments in some cases exceeded 40 monthly wages. The time needed to process the request by the government has been unpredictable, averaging six months and in some cases taking much longer (the procedure involves hearings, in which employers explain their financial performance and business plans to the government to justify the layoffs).

A self-standing, radical reform of the Sri Lankan severance pay system is one option. But because a political decision has been made that the reform of severance pay is contingent on the introduction of unemployment insurance, a difficult question has emerged: should Sri Lanka introduce unemployment insurance? If its introduction brings substantially more flexible employment protection legislation and the design of the system is adjusted to Sri Lanka's circumstances, the answer is yes. But if the unemployment insurance system is costly, if it is not adapted to country circumstances (including the lack of institutional capacity), and if it leaves the existing severance pay essentially intact, the answer is probably no. Such a system would add another protection program to an already privileged group of formal sector workers, and it may reduce labor market performance, thus failing to produce desirable equity and efficiency gains.

Source: Vodopivec (2005).

Unemployment Assistance: How Attractive Is Means-Tested Targeting?

Does targeting of benefits to the most "needy" improve incentives and produce savings? Not necessarily. As Vroman (2002) shows, means testing per se does not ensure that an unemployment benefit system is inexpensive. Depending on the system's parameters—primarily the income-threshold that triggers unemployment assistance—costs can be high, low, or in between.

What are the implications for providing unemployment assistance in developing and transition countries? First, in many of these settings, a potential advantage of unemployment assistance—that eligibility does not require prior contributions— renders such a system nonviable. With large segments of the labor force either underemployed or unemployed, providing an income support system that fails to exclude people without prior work in the formal sector (that is, people who have not paid system contributions) would be fiscally unsustainable. It therefore seems unavoidable that unemployment assistance systems in developing countries base benefit eligibility on the prior payment of system contributions, as is done, for example, under unemployment insurance. Second, due to administrative constraints typically faced by low-income countries, few, if any, of these countries could conduct the required level of monitoring (Vodopivec 2004). Third, abundant informal sector employment opportunities mean that the problem of employment disincentives for other members of the household is more pronounced than in developed countries. If informal sector opportunities abound, ineffective monitoring produces large leakages. Effective monitoring would reduce overall expenditures, but it would impose large administrative costs and perhaps reduce employment and earnings in the informal sector. The applicability of unemployment assistance thus seems limited to countries with relatively developed administrative capacity, a small informal sector, and large fiscal pressures, perhaps as a transition system to unemployment insurance.

Unemployment Insurance Savings Accounts: How Much Insurance Can They Offer?

Among the new approaches to improved income protection of the unemployed, unemployment insurance savings accounts are the most radical, offering the potential to alleviate the moral hazard inherent in traditional unemployment insurance. But, as critics maintain, these accounts do not create the ills of unemployment insurance because they do not provide such insurance in the first place. In its pure form, the system is just a form of forced savings; by its very design it does not pool risk among individuals.[7]

Under certain circumstances, the absence of pooling across individuals may not be critical. Under modest and frequent shocks, as the comprehensive insurance theory of Ehrlic and Becker (1972) suggests, self-insurance through savings may provide adequate smoothing of consumption. Moreover, because the absence of cross-sectional pooling seriously limits the provision of insurance, some unemployment insurance savings account proposals combine individual accounts with public insurance in order to better address large and persistent shocks (Feldstein and Altman 1998; Guasch 1999). For example, under the proposal of Feldstein and Altman, unemployed workers are able to draw benefits monthly, as under the traditional unemployment insurance; the government lends money to accounts when the balance falls below zero (the unemployment insurance savings accounts cum borrowing version). Under such a proposal, the consumption smoothing properties of the unemployment insurance savings accounts system would be no worse than under traditional unemployment insurance, because individuals with negative balances would still receive benefits, as rules of withdrawal would be the same as under the unemployment insurance system. But the savings accounts system would reduce labor market disincentives for workers who end their working careers with positive account balances. This version of the system reduces the gains in terms of reemployment incentives but increases its insurance function.

A similar approach—combining self-insurance and social insurance—is applied in the Chilean unemployment insurance system introduced at the end of 2002. Under the system, employers and workers make contributions to individual savings accounts. Employers and the government contribute to a solidarity fund (employers' contributions reduce their severance payments obligations, so the new unemployment insurance system also partly replaces the severance pay system). To stimulate reemployment, the unemployed first draw benefits from their individual accounts; upon depletion, and subject to the usual unemployment insurance eligibility conditions, they draw from the solidarity fund (Acevedo, Eskenazi, and Pages forthcoming).

What is the rationale for public intervention in unemployment insurance savings accounts? In addressing this question, it is necessary to distinguish between pure unemployment insurance savings accounts and versions that include solidarity funding. The rationale for pure unemployment insurance savings accounts is based largely on country-specific circumstances. These accounts are just a form of self-insurance or forced savings: they support consumption during spells of unemployment by allowing individuals to draw on savings accumulated while working. While the system is likely to generate few inefficiencies, it offers income protection only under very restrictive conditions, such as frequent, modest shocks (short expected durations of unemployment), and it fails to protect some groups of workers (such as workers at the beginning of their working careers, whose accumulations are likely to be low). Such a system could be advocated on the basis that workers are irrational (that they have too high a discount rate or underestimate the risk of becoming unemployed), so that left by themselves they make inadequate provisions for the risk of becoming unemployed.

Pure unemployment insurance savings accounts thus cannot be advocated on the grounds that they correct market failures. But it is possible that they may correct "government failures": such accounts may be justified if they are the only politically palatable solution to reform another badly performing public income support system (such as severance pay) or if the government cannot commit itself not to bail out unprofitable firms in order to avoid politically unacceptable increases in unemployment. Pure unemployment insurance savings accounts may be preferred to traditional unemployment insurance if traditional unemployment insurance creates severe inefficiencies, particularly if the risk of unemployment is frequent and moderate.

In contrast, the rationale for public intervention under the unemployment insurance savings accounts cum borrowing is twofold. First, the system helps smooth consumption by providing access to credit. It thus corrects for capital market imperfections that prevent borrowing against future earnings—a limitation that is often binding in developing countries. Second, this system combines self-insurance with social insurance (because the debt of the workers who end their working lives with negative balances has to be financed through a solidarity fund). The rationale for public intervention is thus widened to include all considerations that underlie the public provision of unemployment insurance. The unemployment insurance savings accounts cum solidarity fund version (such as that adopted in Chile's new system) shares this feature, but its consumption-smoothing capacity is somewhat more limited, as this version does not allow borrowing.

The borrowing version of the scheme potentially offers several advantages. It addresses capital market imperfections, enables widespread risk-pooling, and offers other advantages over the public provision of unemployment insurance (public agencies are better able than private insurers to monitor benefit eligibility, for example). At the same time, the system addresses the moral hazard problem inherent in unemployment insurance by introducing self-policing. This scheme can improve incentives if the self-insurance imposed by individual accounts reduces moral hazard by more than methods applied under traditional unemployment insurance. The scheme can also increase income protection over that provided by pure unemployment insurance savings accounts (or a prefunded severance pay system), because it allows widespread risk-pooling. The system can also increase access to credit, because it allows workers to borrow from their accounts. Simulations by Hopenhayn and Hatchondo (forthcoming) show that when its parameters are appropriately selected, the unemployment insurance savings accounts cum borrowing scheme comes very close to the welfare properties of the optimal unemployment insurance system.

According to some proposals, the efficiency properties of the unemployment insurance savings accounts cum borrowing system can be further improved by combining several risks under one system. Orszag and others (1999) and Yun (2001) propose an integrated unemployment insurance system that would combine unemployment insurance not only with the pension system but also with other systems, such as health, disability, and life insurance. Such a system would integrate intertemporal pooling of various risks of the individual with cross-sectional pooling. By doing so, the system is expected to provide better insurance and significantly reduce disincentives compared with traditional unemployment insurance.

Some design and implementation considerations speak in favor of introducing this system in middle-income and upper-middle-income developing and transition countries. First, weak monitoring capacity in these countries exacerbates the moral hazard problem inherent in traditional unemployment insurance and encourages other misuses of the system. Hence the self-policing nature of the unemployment insurance savings accounts represents a greater advantage. Second, various income support systems exist in developing countries. Their conversion into an unemployment insurance savings accounts-type system could greatly facilitate its introduction. In the Philippines, for example, several mandatory forced savings schemes could, together with severance pay, be merged and transformed into unemployment insurance savings accounts (Esguerra, Ogawa, and Vodopivec 2001). Third, under traditional unemployment insurance, employers in developing countries sometimes fail to contribute to the system. By introducing personal accounts, workers monitor such payments themselves. This feature also makes the accounts less susceptible to political risk. Finally, the administrative complexities of introducing unemployment insurance savings accounts are not prohibitive. The old age insurance systems introduced in many Latin-American countries require similar information systems.[8]

Introducing unemployment insurance savings accounts may create adverse incentive problems of their own, which may be difficult to deal with. First, the system may produce excessive turnover by encouraging workers to choose to become unemployed in order to "get their money back," a problem experienced by the Brazilian severance fund, FGTS (Amadeo, Gill, and Neri 2002). Setting administrative limits on when workers can access funds might help, but doing so would limit labor mobility. Second, unemployment insurance savings accounts cum borrowing may create incentives to "dive and run," that is, it may stimulate workers to borrow and then withdraw from the formal sector and find a job in the informal sector in order to avoid repaying the debt upon reemployment in the formal sector. Conceivably, one could use pension contributions as "collateral" in an integrated unemployment insurance savings accounts–pensions system. But this integration assumes that workers have very long-time horizons, which may not be the case (indeed, if workers had long horizons, they would save for themselves and there would be no need for forced savings mechanisms such as the pure unemployment insurance savings accounts system).

In sum, unemployment insurance savings accounts with solidarity funding—and their variant, the integrated unemployment insurance system—may be promising options, particularly in East Asia and Latin America, where the existence of severance pay systems may ease the transition to unemployment insurance savings accounts. There is a need, however, for further investigation—and piloting—of the system. Too little is known about the working of the scheme to know the types of workers for which, and the conditions under which, the system is likely to work best. Important design parameters of the system (regarding contribution rates and rules for withdrawal, for example) also need to be examined.

Reforming Severance Pay

Severance pay is often considered one of the least appropriate options of income protection: it not only provides inadequate protection, it also imposes efficiency costs by distorting the behavior of firms and workers. Yet except in low-income countries, severance pay is the most prevalent income support system in developing countries. The question of how best to reform existing severance pay systems is thus of obvious importance. Two possible reform directions are examined here. The first is streamlining the system and converting it into a funded system. The second is linking it to unemployment benefit or pension reform.

Streamlining current systems. Countries may have severance pay systems that provoke undesirable responses from firms and workers, impose large monetary and other costs, and are not synchronized with other income protection systems. To streamline their severance pay systems, some countries could simplify system rules. Latin-American countries, for example, could reconsider additional payments imposed for "dismissals without cause" (which almost invariably include economic dismissals). This would not only reduce the costs of the system but also reduce the costs of litigation. Moreover, to reduce unnecessary costs and uncertainty about the ability to lay off workers, the lack of transparency and discretionary nature of severance pay systems in some countries should be addressed. Countries with both social insurance and severance pay systems can reduce costs without reducing insurance by better coordinating payments under the two systems. Unemployment insurance eligibility rules could be adjusted so that insurance benefits would start only after severance benefits "expire," that is, after n months if the individual received n monthly wages as severance payment (such a system is in place in some developed countries, such as Canada). To address the nonperformance of the system, some countries may consider establishing public guarantee funds, thus introducing pooling at the above-firm level.

Prefunding. A more radical reform consists of converting severance pay into a funded system. Such a reform converts conditional obligations to laid-off workers under the traditional severance pay into unconditional obligations to all workers paid regularly to their individual accounts. The reform aims at addressing the nonperformance problem of severance pay, as well as at ameliorating some of the inefficiencies severance pay creates (by, for example, removing obstacles to labor market flows and reducing litigation costs). Conversion would introduce a version of unemployment insurance savings accounts (without solidarity funding).

Prefunding reforms were introduced in Colombia in 1990 and in Austria in 2003. Colombia's system requires employers to deposit a percentage of their workers' wages into guaranteed individual accounts available to workers in the event of job separation (limited access to funds while employed was also foreseen). Kugler (1999, 2002) finds that the reform reduced labor market distortions for two reasons. First, introduction of individual accounts reduced wages; as a result, employment, measured by weekly hours, increased. Wages were reduced as employers shifted 80 percent of the severance payments' costs to workers in the form of lower wages; the total compensation of workers (wages plus deposits to their savings accounts) increased. Second, because the reform removed the discretionary nature of severance payments, both separations and accessions under the new system increased.

Kugler (2002) finds that by transforming uncertain, conditional payments to unconditional payments monitored by a third party (the government), the reform also enhanced the insurance function of the severance pay. Before the reform, nonperformance was a big problem: firms about to go bankrupt could simply not pay severance or negotiate a package substantially below what was owed in severance payments. Thanks to the prefunding requirement, the reform increased the likelihood that workers actually avail themselves of their legal entitlement to severance pay. Among those who received severance payments, consumption smoothing was equally effective before and after the reform.

Austria converted its severance pay to a fully funded contributory system akin to unemployment insurance savings accounts (Koman, Schuh, and Weber forthcoming). The reform extended the entitlement to workers with short tenures and removed obstacles to worker mobility, granting full portability and allowing the accumulation of benefits from the beginning of an employment spell. Employers pay 1.5 percent of workers's salary to them, with resources held in a central account and invested in the capital market. Laid-off workers with job tenure of three years or more can withdraw accumulations in their accounts or keep them and claim them upon retirement. Workers who separate voluntary or have tenures of less than three years are denied the right of immediate withdrawal, a feature that may hinder worker mobility.

Conversion to a funded scheme reduces nonperformance problems, but it only transforms severance pay into a forced savings scheme in which workers insure themselves (self-insurance). One possible further step to improve the insurance function of the system is to add a social insurance component (as a back-up, to minimize disincentives), in order to increase the pooling of the employment risk to the national level.

Advantages of Public Works

Many conditions prevailing in developing countries make public works especially attractive. First, the informal sector is large and pervasive. Informal sector workers do not have access to public income support systems that require social security contributions and thus remain vulnerable to even small income shocks. Second, due to a strong seasonal farm workload, particularly in mono-crop areas, public works can be inexpensively deployed in nonfarm activities in nonpeak periods. The system thus provides an opportunity to productively engage temporary "surplus" labor while minimizing forgone earnings and maximizing poverty reduction effects. Third, the existence of large mono-crop areas makes large segments of the population vulnerable to cyclical and structural shocks. Similar exposure is caused by geographic and climatic shocks. In the absence of market insurance, public works can provide effective insurance in such cases. Fourth, public works do not require complex administration, and they may be quickly set up in areas affected by various shocks. Fifth, obtaining support for public works can benefit from traditions and values that emphasize cooperation and collective support, particularly in rural areas.

Because establishing a program quickly in response to a shock is difficult, public works could be run on a permanent basis (as employment guarantee schemes). Experience shows that public works in transition countries do not increase employability and may stigmatize participants, so this option is less desirable in these countries.

National Income Level and the Choice of Program

One size does not fit all. An unemployment support program suitable for one group of countries may not fit the institutional or other characteristics of another group. How should a country with a certain set of characteristics choose an unemployment support program?

The preferred choices of unemployment support by groups of countries are summarized in table 2.[9] For low-income countries, public works is the program of choice, particularly because the program is effective in combating poverty. Other programs are much less suitable. Unemployment insurance is not appropriate in low-income countries, because they lack the necessary administrative capacity, their labor markets are largely informal, and funds set aside for this program may be subject to political risk. Reducing overly generous severance pay benefits sometimes found in low-income countries would help reduce labor market duality.

Similar considerations suggest that public works are the preferred scheme in lower-middle-income countries. Depending on circumstances, however, a simplified social insurance program, offering modest benefits, may be appropriate. Such a scheme may be necessary to pave the way to overhauling an outdated severance pay system (see box 1). Given the weak administrative capacity of lower-middle-income countries, unemployment insurance savings account cum solidarity funding seems particularly desirable.

Other existing institutions may also affect the choice of the unemployment support programs. For example, a country with a provident fund allowing preretirement withdrawals (for housing or education, for example) may introduce unemployment income support by simply expanding the set of contingencies financed by such a fund. With their greater administrative capacity, transition countries may opt for unemployment assistance, in order to improve the targeting of benefits, but unemployment assistance should base benefit eligibility on the payment of contributions to ensure fiscal sustainability.

The program of choice for upper-middle-income countries is unemployment insurance, combined with other labor market programs. These countries should introduce unemployment insurance cautiously, starting with modest benefits and simple rules. To increase their generosity and thus their consumption-smoothing function, unemployment insurance should gradually improve the monitoring of benefit eligibility (by, for example, interlinking administrative information systems) and help beneficiaries improve their employability. To avoid perverse incentives,

Table 2. Recommended Public Unemployment Support Programs, by Country Income Level

Country Income Group	Recommended Unemployment Support Program	Objectives Served	Critical Conditions and Considerations Supporting Recommendation
Low income	• Public works • Reduced severance pay benefits (if overly generous)	• Reduces poverty • Provides goods and services to the poor • Spurs community development and empowerment • Reduces labor market duality	• Low administrative capacity, high labor market informality, and high political risk make this group unsuitable for unemployment insurance programs
Lower middle income	• Public works • Simplified, modest, adapted social insurance program (unemployment insurance, unemployment assistance, or unemployment insurance savings account cum solidarity funding), depending on circumstances	• Reduces poverty • Provides goods and services to the poor • Spurs community development and empowerment • Paves the way to reduce labor market duality	• Introduction of a social insurance should be conditional on improving other programs (by cutting back excessive, nontransparent severance pay systems, for example, thereby moving from job to income protection) • To avoid perverse incentives and given the weak administrative capacity of lower-middle-income countries, unemployment insurance savings account cum solidarity funding may be desirable • Unemployment assistance may be suitable for transition countries that have better administrative capacity and can thus target the poor more effectively; eligibility should be based on previous contributions to the program

(Continued)

Table 2. Continued

Country Income Group	Recommended Unemployment Support Program	Objectives Served	Critical Conditions and Considerations Supporting Recommendation
Upper middle income	• Social insurance programs (unemployment insurance, unemployment assistance, unemployment insurance savings accounts), combined with other programs	• Smoothes consumption • Makes job search more efficient	• Experience and better integration of public information systems may lead to the increased sophistication of social insurance programs • To avoid perverse incentives, unemployment insurance savings account cum solidarity funding may be desirable
High income	• Unemployment insurance, supplemented by labor market and other programs (public works, training, social assistance)	• Smoothes consumption • Makes job search more efficient • Helps marginalized workers retain labor force attachment and improve employability • Reduces income inequalities and counters social exclusion	• Unemployment insurance relies on strong administrative capacity to monitor benefit eligibility • Particularly suitable for highly formalized labor markets

unemployment insurance savings account cum solidarity funding may also be desirable for this group of countries.

In addition to providing unemployment insurance with a high level of consumption smoothing (and extending assistance upon its expiration as a social assistance benefit), high-income countries offer a full range of active labor market programs to the unemployed. These programs include job search assistance, training, public works, youth unemployment programs, and often also employment subsidy programs.

Adapting the System and Offering a Mix of Options

Institutional and other characteristics of developing and transition countries strongly affect not only the choice but also the design of income support system as well as the mix of options offered. This section describes desirable design adjustments of unemployment insurance and explains why the simultaneous provision of several systems may be desirable.

Adjusting Unemployment Insurance to Developing Countries

When introducing unemployment insurance outside developed countries, how should the system be adjusted to enhance its protection while minimizing its negative effects on incentives and efficiency? Two key features of developing countries that influence the design of unemployment insurance need to be taken into accounted: the level of administrative capacity, which is lower than in developed countries, and the abundant opportunities to work in the informal sector. The example of Sri Lanka is instructive. Sri Lanka lacks the administration capacity to effectively implement a Western-style unemployment insurance. Employment offices were established in Sri Lanka only in 2003, when 17 regional centers providing job-matching services were opened (Vodopivec 2005). Many activities, particularly effective monitoring of continuing eligibility, could be carried out properly only in the medium to long term.[10] Moreover, the informal sector, which employs more than half the country's workforce, offers abundant opportunities for work that are hard to monitor and record.[11]

The following design features are especially desirable to accommodate these country-specific circumstances. First, to minimize disincentives, both the level and duration of benefits should be limited. Flat-rate benefits are particularly appealing, because they are simpler to administer and offer fewer possibilities for misuse and fraud. Another option is declining benefits during individual unemployment spells. Second, continuing eligibility criteria need to be adjusted. Argentina's unemployment insurance system has completely forgone the monitoring of continuing eligibility—a decision Argentina may reconsider once it develops sufficient monitoring capacity (the absence of monitoring continuing eligibility reinforces the need to offer modest benefits). Third, social insurance could be combined with self-insurance, following the approach of the new Chilean unemployment insurance system in order to reduce labor market disincentives.

Offering a Well-Balanced, Flexible Mix of Options

To satisfy diverse needs and objectives, and to confront various types of risks, countries should offer a well-balanced, flexible mix of income protection systems and complement them with systems outside income protection. There are several reasons to offer a mix of income support systems rather than a single system. Different systems have different objectives. The primary goal of some systems is to compensate for the loss of earnings; other systems and policies may emphasize human resource development. In some stages, the labor reallocation goal may deserve special attention (transition countries are a case in point). Moreover, diverse groups of workers have different needs. Important segments of the workforce in developing countries are engaged in the informal sector and are thus ineligible for social insurance systems and severance pay. Government should provide supplemental income support systems in which anyone can participate (programs such as public works and training). Supplemental systems may be dictated by the regional unevenness of the size of private transfers. Regions that receive lower levels of remittances from abroad, for example, should have wider opportunities for public works.

Another reason for offering a mix of systems is that they differ in their ability to confront shocks. The selection of systems should take into account the prevalence and severity of shocks typically confronted. For example, the effectiveness of unemployment insurance is reduced during recessions, so supplemental systems (such as public works, training, or conditional cash transfers) may be needed. Similarly, in dealing with industry-level risks, special redundancy systems may be put in place to promote enterprise restructuring. The occurrence of natural disasters points to the need for flexible, quickly deployable systems (such as public works).

Countries should also complement income support with systems in other areas, including labor market and financial policies. Well-functioning labor, insurance, and financial markets can substantially increase opportunities for self-protection (by reducing the risk of unemployment) and self-insurance (by contributing to short unemployment spells).

Income support can often be effectively complemented by active labor market programs (training, employment subsidies, job search assistance, promotion of self-employment, youth programs). Depending on a country's fiscal position, objectives, and conditions, these efforts may be used to promote employment opportunities of the unemployed. Two aspects of interaction with income support systems are worth mentioning. First, active programs should be coordinated with income support systems, in order to minimize perverse incentives for enrollment in active programs and weaken incentives for reemployment. Second, active labor market programs may be used as a screening device for participants of income support systems.

Another important complementary program is conditional cash transfers, such as Mexico's PROGRESA and Brazil's PETI. To increase educational attainment and improve health, these transfers help poor families pay for basic health and schooling expenses, as long as their children regularly visit health clinics and attend school. These programs discourage counterproductive coping mechanisms, such as reducing healthcare expenditures and taking children out of school. Evaluations show that these programs can raise school enrollment and attendance rates and improve child health and nutrition (Rawlings and Rubio 2003). They undoubtedly reduce poverty in the longer run.

Diverse needs and circumstances also call for creative, innovative programs. One important example is social funds. Social funds are agencies that finance small-scale projects, predominantly in poor communities. To ensure that truly valuable projects are selected, the communities themselves identify and partly finance projects. Social funds demonstrate the ability to foster cooperation among local actors, provide valuable products and services to vulnerable segments of population, and engage the poor in the implementation of projects, thereby providing them with income protection (Rawlings, Sheburne-Benz, and Van Domelen 2003).

Summary

Each system of income support for the unemployed has its strengths and its weaknesses.

- Unemployment insurance facilitates a high degree of consumption smoothing, performs well under various types of shocks, and acts as an automatic macroeconomic stabilizer, but it creates reemployment disincentives and wage pressures, which increase the equilibrium unemployment rate and make unemployment persistent. Because its successful performance relies on conditions that are typically lacking in developing and transition countries, the case for introducing unemployment insurance is less compelling in these countries than in developed countries.
- Unemployment assistance allows more effective targeting, but it may not yield savings over unemployment insurance. It provides a lower level of protection for high-income workers, is more expensive to administer than unemployment insurance, and creates similar employment disincentives. Its applicability is thus limited, perhaps to countries with relatively developed administrative capacity and a small informal sector.

- By internalizing the costs of unemployment benefits, unemployment insurance savings accounts ameliorate the moral hazard inherent in traditional unemployment insurance and thus improve reemployment incentives. Given the weak monitoring capacity of developing countries, this is an important advantage. When integrated version with social insurance, which pools risk across participants, the system may improve work incentives while in principle offering income protection similar to that of traditional unemployment insurance. The scheme also has the potential to attract informal sector workers. By allowing individuals to borrow from their accounts, however, some versions of integrated accounts create incentives to withdraw from a formal sector in order to avoid repaying the debt. Because the system has been largely untested, further investigation of its effects and design parameters, including piloting of the system, is needed.

- Severance pay is an important option because it is already provided in many developing and transition countries. It offers few advantages, however. To improve its protection and efficiency effects, countries may consider streamlining these systems and reducing their costs if they are too generous. A more radical reform could introduce prefunding, to improve nonperformance and ameliorate labor market rigidities.

- Public works program are effective in reaching the poor, have good targeting properties and substantial capacity to redistribute income from the rich to the poor, are able to attract informal sector workers, can provide a flexible and fast response to shocks, and are administratively less demanding than other public income support systems. Although public works also have high nonwage costs, are likely to have a countercyclical pattern of funding, and may stigmatize participants, they are suitable for developing countries, particularly as a complementary program.

Notes

Milan Vodopivec is a senior economist in the Social Protection Unit, Human Development Network, South Asia Region at the World Bank. His e-mail address is mvodopivec@worldbank.org. This article draws heavily on Vodopivec (2004). It is part of a larger effort by the World Bank's Labor Market Group, Human Development Network, to understand better and synthesize the effects of labor market policies and programs.

1. For a recent summary of the efficiency effects of unemployment insurance as well as other key income support programs, see Vodopivec (2004).

2. While the association between more generous benefits and longer durations of unemployment has long been established, recent empirical studies also persuasively show that more generous unemployment benefits cause exits from unemployment to slow down (see, for example, van Ours and Vodopived forthcoming).

3. Several transition countries ran deficits financed out of state budgets in the 1990s (Vodopivec, Wörgötter, and Raju 2005).

4. For an excellent review and evaluation of unemployment insurance savings accounts in Latin-American countries, see Ferrer and Riddell (forthcoming).

5. Coady, Grosch, and Hoddinott (2004) compare four targeting methods: individual assessment (based on means testing or "proxy means testing," that is, construction of a targeting index from income and wealth attributes); categorical targeting (such as child allowances); self-selection methods (such as public works and food subsidies); and community assessment.

6. Coady, Grosch, and Hoddinott (2004) find that community involvement in some countries does help improve targeting. In contrast, Galasso and Ravallion (2005) find evidence that the more unequal distribution of assets in a village, the better positioned the nonpoor are to capture the benefits of the program.

7. For a careful analysis of different unemployment insurance savings account designs and their effects on protection and efficiency, see Parsons (forthcoming).

8. Smetters (2000) assesses the risk of having high rather than low to medium administrative costs of private pension accounts in the United States. A similar assessment is valid for unemployment insurance savings accounts and for other countries. To keep the costs of private accounts low, Smetters proposes that investment funds be approved and regulated by the government and subject to standard auditing controls to reduce fraud. He also proposes limits on investment charges and on the free movement of money between funds. In such a case, most of the administrative costs would come from collecting contributions from individual workers, at few extra costs compared with the public system.

9. Countries are grouped by per capita income, a proxy for key institutional and labor market conditions.

10. To affect the unemployment insurance system, the following administrative procedures would have to be put in place: making, assessing, and approving claims for compensation; making payments to approved claimants; monitoring the continuing eligibility of beneficiaries; providing employment and training services to beneficiaries; and auditing, monitoring, and evaluating the system.

11. Other factors are susceptibility to political risk (for example, the danger of using unemployment insurance funds for other purposes) and the nature of collective bargaining (under fragmented bargaining, the introduction of unemployment insurance is more likely to generate wage pressures). See Vodopivec (2004).

References

Acemoglu, D., and R. Shimer. 1999. "Efficient Unemployment Insurance." *Journal of Political Economy* 107 (5): 893–928.

———. 2000. "Productivity Gains from Unemployment Insurance." *European Economic Review* 44 (7): 1195–1224.

Acevedo, G., P. Eskenazi, and C. Pages. Forthcoming. "The Chilean Unemployment Insurance: A New Model of Income Support for the Unemployed?" In R. Holzmann and M. Vodopivec, eds, *Improving Severance Pay: An International Perspective*. World Bank, Washington, D.C.

Amadeo, E. J., I. S. Gill, and M. C. Neri. 2002. "Assessing the Impact of Regulations on Informal Workers in Brazil." In I.S. Gill, C.E. Montenegro, and D. Domeland, eds, *Crafting Labor Policy: Techniques and Lessons from Latin America*. World Bank, Washington, D.C.

Atkinson, A. B. 1995a. *Incomes and the Welfare State: Essays on Britain and Europe*. Cambridge: Cambridge University Press.

———. 1995b. "On Targeting Social Security: Theory and Western Experience with Family Benefits." In D. van de Walle and K. Nead, eds, *Public Spending and the Poor: Theory and Evidence*. Baltimore, Md.: John Hopkins University Press.

Atkinson, A. B., and J. Micklewright. 1991. "Unemployment Compensation and Labor Market Transitions: A Critical Review." *Journal of Economic Literature* 29 (4): 1679–1727.

Attanasio, O., and J. V. Rios-Rull. 2000. "Consumption Smoothing in Island Economies: Can Public Insurance Reduce Welfare?" *European Economic Review* 44 (7): 1225–58.

Beegle, K., E. Frankenberg, and D. Thomas. 1999. "Measuring Change in Indonesia." Labor and Population Program Working Paper Series 99–07. RAND, Santa Monica, Calif.

Besley, T., and R. Burgess. 2004. "Can Labor Regulation Hinder Economic Performance? Evidence from India." *Quarterly Journal of Economics* 119 (1): 91–134.

Betcherman, G., and R. Islam. 2001. *East Asian Labor Market and the Economic Crisis: Impacts, Responses, and Lessons.* World Bank, Washington, D.C.

Betcherman, G., K. Olivas, and A. Dar. 2004. "Impacts of Active Labor Market Programs: New Evidence from Evaluations with Particular Attention to Developing and Transition Countries." Social Protection Discussion Paper Series 0402. World Bank, Washington, D.C.

Blanchard, O. 2000. "The Economics of Unemployment: Shocks, Institutions, and Interactions." Lionel Robbins Lectures, London School of Economics. [http://econ-www.mit.edu/faculty/download_pdf.php?id=800].

Blanchard, O., and J. Wolfers. 2000. "The Role of Shocks and Institutions in the Rise in. European Unemployment: the Aggregate Evidence." *Economic Journal* 110 (462): 1–33.

Boone, P., P. Fredriksson, B. Holmlund, and J. van Ours. 2001. "Optimal Unemployment Insurance with Monitoring and Sanctions." Discussion Paper 3082. Centre for Economic Policy Research, London.

Botero, J., S. Djankov, R. La Porta, F. Lopez-de-Silanes, and A. Shleifer. 2002. *The Regulation of Labor.* NBER Working Paper 9756. Cambridge, Mass.: National Bureau of Economic Research.

Chimerine, T., T. S. Black, and L. Coffey. 1999. "Unemployment Insurance as an Economic Stabilizer: Evidence of Effectiveness over Three Decades." *Unemployment Insurance Occasional Paper* 99–8. U.S. Department of Labor, Washington, D.C.

Coady, D., M. Grosch, and J. Hoddinott. 2004. *The Targeting of Transfers in Developing Countries: Review of Experiences and Lessons.* World Bank, Washington, D.C.

Davis, S., and J. Haltiwanger. 1999. "Gross Job Flows." In Orley Ashenfelter and David Card, eds, *Handbook of Labor Economics.* Amsterdam: North Holland.

De Ferranti, D., G. E. Perry, I. S. Gill, and L. Serven. 2000. *Securing Our Future in a Global Economy.* World Bank Latin and Caribbean Studies. World Bank, Washington, D.C.

Dungan, P., and S. Murphy. 1995. "The UI System as an Automatic Stabilizer in Canada." Human Resources Development Canada, Hull, Quebec.

Ehrlic, I., and G. Becker. 1972. "Market Insurance, Self-Insurance, and Self-Protection." *Journal of Political Economy* 80 (4): 623–48.

Esguerra, J., M. Ogawa, and M. Vodopivec. 2001. "Options of Public Income Support for the Unemployed in the Philippines." *Philippine Review of Economics* 38 (2): 37–66.

Fallon, P. R., and R. E. B. Lucas. 1991. "The Impact of Changes in Job Security Regulations in India and Zimbabwe." *World Bank Economic Review* 5 (1): 395–413.

Feldstein, M., and D. Altman. 1998. *Unemployment Insurance Savings Accounts.* NBER Working Paper 6860. Cambridge, Mass.: National Bureau of Economic Research.

Ferrer, A., and C. W. Riddell. Forthcoming. "Unemployment Insurance Savings Accounts in Latin America: Overview and Assessment." In R. Holzmann and M. Vodopivec, eds, *Improving Severance Pay: An International Perspective.* World Bank, Washington, D.C.

Forster, M. 2000. "Trends and Driving Factors in Income Distribution and Poverty in the OECD Area." *OECD Labour Market and Social Policy Occasional Paper* No. 42, Paris.

Galasso, E., and M. Ravallion. 2005. "Decentralized Targeting of an Anti-Poverty Program." *Journal of Public Economics. Journal of Public Economics* 89 (4): 705–27.

Gill, I. S., and N. Ilahi. 2000. "Economic Insecurity, Individual Behavior and Social Policy." Paper prepared for the Regional Study "Managing Economic Insecurity in Latin America and the Caribbean." World Bank, Washington, D.C.

Gruber, J. 1997. "Consumption-Smoothing Effects of Unemployment Insurance." *American Economic Review* 87 (1): 192–205.

Guasch, J. L. 1999. "An Alternative to Traditional Unemployment Insurance Programs: A Liquidity-Based Approach against the Risk of Earnings Losses." World Bank, Latin America and Caribbean Region, Finance, Private Sector, and Infrastructure, Washington, D.C.

Haddad, L., and M. Adato. 2001. "How Efficiently Do Public Works Programs Transfer Benefits to the Poor? Evidence from South Africa." FCND DP 108. International Food Policy Research Institute, Washington, D.C.

Haffner, R., S. Nickell, G. Nicoletti, S. Scarpetta, and G. Zoega. 2001. "European Integration, Liberalization and Labour Market Performance." In G. Bertola, T. Boeri, and G. Nicoletti, eds, *Welfare and Employment in a United Europe*. Cambridge, Mass.: MIT Press.

Haltiwanger, J, S. Scarpetta, and M. Vodopivec. 2003. "How Institutions Affect Labor Market Outcomes: Evidence from Transition Countries." Paper presented at the World Bank Economists Forum. Washington, D.C., April.

Hamermesh, D. S. 1992. "Unemployment Insurance for Developing Countries." World Bank Policy Research Working Paper No. 897. Washington, D.C.

Hamermesh, D. S., and D. T. Slesnick. 1995. *Unemployment Insurance and Household Welfare: Microeconomic Evidence 1980–93*. NBER Working Paper 5315. Cambridge, Mass.: National Bureau of Economic Research.

Heckman, J. J., and C. Pages. 2000. *The Cost of Job Security Regulation: Evidence from Latin American Labor Markets*. NBER Working Paper 7773. Cambridge, Mass.: National Bureau of Economic Research.

Holmlund, B. 1998. "Unemployment Insurance in Theory and Practice." *Scandinavian Journal of Economics* 100 (1): 113–41.

Holzmann, R., K. Iyer, and M. Vodopivec. Forthcoming. "Severance Pay Programs around the World: Rationale, Status, and Reforms." In R. Holzmann and M. Vodopivec, eds, *Improving Severance Pay: An International Perspective*. World Bank, Washington, D.C.

Hopenhayn, H., and J. C. Hatchondo. Forthcoming. "The Welfare Consequences of Alternative Designs of Unemployment Insurance Savings Accounts." In R. Holzmann and M. Vodopivec, eds, *Improving Severance Pay: An International Perspective*. World Bank, Washington, D.C.

ILO (International Labour Organization). 2001. LABORSTA. Geneva: International Labour Office.

Koman, R., U. Schuh, and A. Weber. Forthcoming. "The Austrian Severance Payments Reform: Toward a Funded Pension Pillar." In R. Holzmann and M. Vodopivec, eds, *Improving Severance Pay: An International Perspective*. World Bank, Washington, D.C.

Kugler, A. 1999. "The Impact of Firing Costs on Turnover and Unemployment: Evidence from the Colombian Labour Market Reform." *International Tax and Public Finance Journal* 6 (3): 389–410.

———. 2002. "From Severance Pay to Self-Insurance: Effects of Severance Payments Savings Accounts in Colombia." IZA DP No. 434, Institute for the Study of Labor, Bonn, Germany.

Lazear, E. P. 1990. "Job Security Provisions and Employment." *Quarterly Journal of Economics* 105 (3): 699–726.

Lipsett, B. 1999. "Supporting Workers in Transition: Income Support Programs for the Unemployed in Brazil and Argentina." Paper prepared for the World Bank, Human Development Network, Washington, D.C.

MacIsaac, D., and M. Rama. 2000. "Mandatory Severance Pay in Peru: An Assessment of Its Coverage and Effects Using Panel Data." World Bank, Development Research Group, Public Service Delivery, Washington, D.C.

Mansor, N., T. E. Chye, A. Boehanoeddin, F. Said, and S. M. Said. 2001. "Malaysia: Protecting Workers and Fostering Growth." In G. Betcherman and R. Islam, eds, *East Asian Labor Market and the Economic Crisis: Impacts, Responses, and Lessons*. World Bank, Washington, D.C.

Marquez, G. 1999. "Labor Markets and Income Support: What Did We Learn from the Crisis?" Inter-American Development Bank, Office of the Chief Economist, Washington, D.C.

Mazza, J. 1999. "Unemployment Insurance: Case Studies and Lessons for Latin America and the Caribbean." Technical Study RE2/SO2, Inter-American Development Bank, Washington, D.C.

OECD (Organisation for Economic Co-operation and Development). 1999. *Employment Outlook*. Paris.

———. 2000. *Employment Outlook*. Paris.

Orszag, J. M., P. R. Orszag, D. J. Snower, and J. E. Stiglitz. 1999. "The Impact of Individual Accounts: Piecemeal vs. Comprehensive Approaches." Paper presented at the Annual Bank Conference on Development Economics, World Bank, Washington, D.C., April 29.

Parsons, D. Forthcoming. "Savings Accounts as an Alternative to Job Separation Pay: Theoretical Considerations." In R. Holzmann and M. Vodopivec, eds, *Improving Severance Pay: An International Perspective*. World Bank, Washington, D.C.

Ravallion, M. 1991. "Reaching the Rural Poor through Public Employment: Arguments, Evidence, and Lessons from South Asia." *World Bank Research Observer* 6 (2): 153–75.

———. 1999. "Appraising Workfare." *World Bank Research Observer* 14 (1): 31–48.

Rawlings, L. B., and G. M. Rubio. 2003. "Evaluating the Impact of Conditional Transfer Programs: Lessons from Latin America." Policy Research Working Paper 3119. World Bank, Washington, D.C.

Rawlings, L. B., L. Sheburne-Benz, and J. Van Domelen. 2003. *Evaluating Social Funds: A Cross-Country Analysis of Community Investments*. World Bank, Washington, D.C.

Smetters, K. 2000. "The Design and Cost of Pension Guarantees." Brookings/SIEPR/TIAA-CREF Conference on Public Policies and Private Pensions, Washington, D.C., September.

Subbarao, K. 1997. "Public Works as an Anti-Poverty Program: An Overview of Cross-Country Experience." *American Journal of Agricultural Economics* 79 (2): 678–83.

———. 2003. "Systemic Shocks and Social Protection: Role and Effectiveness of Public Works Programs." Social Protection Discussion Paper 0302. World Bank, Washington, D.C.

U.S. Social Security Administration. 1999. *Social Security Programs throughout the World: 1999*. Washington, D.C.

———. 2002a. *Social Security Programs throughout the World: Asia and the Pacific 2002*. Washington, D.C. [www.ssa.gov/policy/docs/progdesc/ssptw/2002-2003/asia/index.html].

———. 2002b. *Social Security Programs throughout the World: Europe*. Washington, D.C. [www.ssa.gov/policy/docs/progdesc/ssptw/2002-2003/europe/index.html].

van Ours, J., and M. Vodopivec. Forthcoming. "How Shortening the Potential Duration of Unemployment Benefits Affects the Duration of Unemployment: Evidence from a Natural Experiment." *Journal of Labor Economics*.

Vodopivec, M. 2004. *Income Support for the Unemployed: Issues and Options*. World Bank, Washington, D.C.

———. 2005. "Introducing Unemployment Insurance in Sri Lanka." World Bank, Human Development Network, South Asia Region, Washington, D.C.

Vodopivec, M., and T. Rejec. Forthcoming. "Unemployment Insurance Savings Accounts: Simulation Results for Estonia." In R. Holzmann and M. Vodopivec, eds, *Improving Severance Pay: An International Perspective*. World Bank, Washington, D.C.

Vodopivec, M., A. Wörgötter, and D. Raju. 2005. "Unemployment Benefit Systems in Central and Eastern Europe: A Review of the 1990s." *Comparative Economic Studies* 47 (4): 615–51.

Vroman, W. 2002. "Unemployment Insurance and Unemployment Assistance: A Comparison." Social Protection Discussion Paper 0203. World Bank and Urban Institute, Washington, D.C.

Wodon, Q. 2000. *Poverty and Policy in Latin America and the Caribbean.* World Bank Technical Paper 46. Washington, D.C.

World Bank. 2003. World Development Indicators and Global Development Finance central database. Washington, D.C.

Yoo, K. S. 2001. "The Feasibility of Introducing an Employment Insurance Scheme in the Philippines." Paper prepared for the World Bank–International Labour Organization–Japanese Ministry of Labor–Philippine Department of Labor and Employment seminar on "Labor Market Policies: Their Implications for East and South East Asia." March 1–2, Manila.

Yun, J. 2001. "On the Integration of Unemployment Insurance with Pension through Individual Savings Account." World Bank, Human Development Network, Washington, D.C.

Corporate Governance and Development

Stijn Claessens

The literature shows that good corporate governance generally pays—for firms, for markets, and for countries. It is associated with a lower cost of capital, higher returns on equity, greater efficiency, and more favorable treatment of all stakeholders, although the direction of causality is not always clear. The law and finance literature has documented the important role of institutions aimed at contractual and legal enforcement, including corporate governance, across countries. Using firm-level data, researchers have documented relationships between countries' corporate governance frameworks on the one hand and performance, valuation, the cost of capital, and access to external financing on the other. Given the benefits of good corporate governance, firms and countries should voluntarily reform more. Resistance by entrenched owners and managers at the firm level and political economy factors at the level of markets and countries partly explain why they do not.

Corporate governance, a phrase that not long ago meant little to all but a handful of scholars and shareholders, has now become a mainstream concern—a staple of discussion in corporate boardrooms, academic meetings, and policy circles around the globe. Two events are responsible for the heightened interest in corporate governance. During the wave of financial crises in 1998 in the Russian Federation, Asia, and Brazil, the behavior of the corporate sector affected all the economies, and deficiencies in corporate governance endangered the stability of the global financial system. Just three years later, confidence in the corporate sector was sapped by corporate governance scandals in the United States and Europe that triggered some of the largest insolvencies in history. In the aftermath, not only has the phrase *corporate governance* become nearly a household term, but economists, the corporate world, and policymakers everywhere have begun to recognize the potential macroeconomic consequences of weak corporate governance systems.

The scandals and crises, however, are just manifestations of a number of structural reasons why corporate governance has become more important for economic development and well-being (Becht, Bolton, and Roell 2003). The private, market-based

© The Author 2006. Published by Oxford University Press on behalf of the International Bank for Reconstruction and Development / THE WORLD BANK. All rights reserved. For permissions, please e-mail: journals.permissions@oxfordjournals.org.
doi:10.1093/wbro/lkj004   Advance Access publication 23 February 2006   21:91–122

investment process is now much more important for most economies than it used to be, and that process is underpinned by better corporate governance. With the size of firms increasing and the role of financial intermediaries and institutional investors growing, the mobilization of capital has increasingly become one step removed from the principal owner. At the same time, the allocation of capital has become more complex, as investment choices have widened with the opening up and liberalization of financial and real markets and as structural reforms, including price deregulation and increased competition, have increased companies' exposure to market forces and risks. These developments have made the monitoring of the use of capital more complex in certain ways, enhancing the need for good corporate governance.

This article traces the many dimensions through which corporate governance works in firms and countries. It reviews the extensive literature on the subject and identifies areas where more study is needed. A well-established body of research has for some time acknowledged the increased importance of legal foundations, including the quality of the corporate governance framework, for economic development and well-being. Research has started to address the links between law and economics, highlighting the role of legal foundations and well-defined property rights for the functioning of market economies. This literature has also started to address the importance and impact of corporate governance.[1]

Some of this material is not easily accessible to the non-academic. Much of it refers to developed countries, in particular the United States. Furthermore, this literature does not always focus on the relationship between corporate governance and economic development and well-being. The purpose of this article is to fill these gaps.

The article is structured as follows. It starts by defining corporate governance, as that determines the scope of the issues addressed; reviewing how corporate governance can be and has been defined; and explaining why more attention is being paid to corporate governance in particular and to protection of private property rights more generally. It then explores why corporate governance may matter, by reviewing the evidence of the effects of property rights on financial development and growth. It also provides some background on ownership patterns around the world that determine and affect the scope and nature of corporate governance problems. After analyzing what the literature has to say about the various channels through which corporate governance affects economic development and well-being, the article reviews the empirical facts about some of these relationships. It explores recent research documenting how legal aspects can affect firm valuation, influence the degree of corporate governance problems, and more broadly affect firm performance and financial structure. The article concludes by identifying some main policy and research issues that require further study.

What Is Corporate Governance and Why Is It Receiving More Attention?

Before explaining why more attention is being paid to corporate governance, one needs a definition of corporate governance. Defining the concept is not obvious, as corporate governance can be, and has been, defined in different ways. One also needs to clarify how corporate governance relates to the protection of private property rights more generally.

What Is Corporate Governance?

Definitions of corporate governance vary widely. They tend to fall into two categories. The first set of definitions is concerned with a set of behavioral patterns—the actual behavior of corporations, in terms of such measures as performance, efficiency, growth, financial structure, and treatment of shareholders and other stakeholders. The second set is concerned with the normative framework—the rules under which firms are operating, with the rules coming from such sources as the legal system, the judicial system, financial markets, and factor (labor) markets.

For studies of single countries or firms within a country, the first type of definition represents the more logical choice. It considers such matters as how boards of directors operate, the role of executive compensation in determining firm performance, the relationship between labor policies and firm performance, and the role of multiple shareholders. The associated analysis is interested largely in the mechanisms through which corporate governance is exercised. [Becht, Bolton, and Roell (2003) provide a general discussion of the various corporate governance mechanisms; Claessens and Berglöf (in this issue) use their classification to analyze enforcement.]

For comparative studies, the second type of definition is more logical. It investigates how differences in the normative framework affect the behavioral patterns of firms, investors, and others and analyzes how countries' legal and institutional framework shapes the use of various corporate governance mechanisms.

In a comparative review, the question of how broadly to define the framework for corporate governance arises. Under a narrow definition, the focus would be only on the rules in capital markets governing equity investments in publicly listed firms. This would include listing requirements, insider dealing arrangements, disclosure and accounting rules, and protection of minority shareholder rights.

Under a definition more specific to the provision of finance, the focus would be on how outside investors protect themselves against expropriation by insiders. This would include protections of minority rights and the strength of creditor rights, as reflected in collateral and bankruptcy laws. It could also include such issues as the composition and rights of executive directors and the ability to pursue class action suits. This definition is close to the one advanced by Shleifer and Vishny (1997) in their seminal review: "Corporate governance deals with the ways in which suppliers of finance to corporations assure themselves of getting a return on their investment" (p. 737). This definition can be expanded to address the various types of suppliers of finance. One can then define corporate governance as being concerned with the resolution of collective action problems among dispersed investors and the reconciliation of conflicts of interest among various corporate claimholders.

A broader definition would be to define corporate governance as a set of mechanisms through which firms operate when ownership is separated from management. This is close to the definition used by Sir Adrian Cadbury, the former head of the Committee on the Financial Aspects of Corporate Governance in the United Kingdom: "Corporate governance is the system by which companies are directed and controlled" (Cadbury Committee 1992).

An even broader definition is to define a governance system as "the complex set of constraints that shape the ex post bargaining over the quasi rents generated by the firm" (Zingales 1998, p. 499). This definition focuses on the division of claims; it can be expanded to include the complex set of constraints that determine the quasi-rents (profits) generated by the firm in the course of relationships and to shape the ex post bargaining over them. This definition refers to both the determination of value added by firms and the allocation of it among stakeholders that have relationships with the firm. It can be read to refer to a set of rules as well as to institutions.

Corresponding to this broad definition, the objective of a good corporate governance framework would be to maximize the contribution of firms to the overall economy, including all stakeholders. Under this definition, corporate governance would include the relationship between shareholders, creditors, and corporations; between financial markets, institutions, and corporations; and between employees and corporations. Corporate governance could also encompass corporate social responsibility, including such aspects as the firm's dealings with respect to culture and the environment.

When analyzing corporate governance in a cross-country perspective, the question of whether the framework extends to rules or institutions arises. Two views have been advanced. One is that the framework is determined by rules and by markets and outsiders. This view has prevailed in and been applied to Anglo-Saxon countries. In much of the rest of the world, institutions—specifically, banks and insiders—are thought to determine the actual corporate governance framework.

In reality, both institutions and rules matter, and the distinction between the two can be misleading. Moreover, both institutions and rules evolve over time. Institutions do not arise in a vacuum; they are affected by the rules in the country or the world. Similarly, laws and rules are affected by a country's institutional setup. In the end, both institutions and rules are endogenous to other factors and conditions in the country. Among these, ownership structures and the role of the state matter for the evolution of institutions and rules through the political economy process. Shleifer and Vishny (1997, p. 738) take a dynamic perspective stating that "corporate governance mechanisms are economic and legal institutions that can be altered through political process." This dynamic aspect is very relevant in a cross-country review, but it has received relatively little attention from researchers.

When considering both institutions and rules, it is easy to become bewildered by the scope of institutions and rules that may matter. An easier way to understand what corporate governance means is to take the functional approach. This approach recognizes that financial services come in many forms but that if the services are unbundled, most, if not all, key elements are similar (Bodie and Merton 1995). This line of analysis of the functions rather than the specific products provided by financial institutions and markets distinguishes six types of functions: pooling resources and subdividing shares, transferring resources across time and space, managing risk, generating and providing information, dealing with incentive problems, and resolving competing claims on the wealth generated by the corporation. One can define corporate governance mechanisms as the range of institutions and policies that are involved in these functions as they relate to corporations. Both markets and institutions will, for example, affect the way the corporate governance function of generating and providing high-quality and transparent information is performed.

Why Has Corporate Governance Received More Attention Lately?

One reason why corporate governance has recently received more attention is the proliferation of scandals and crises. These scandals and crises are just manifestations of a number of structural reasons why corporate governance has become more important for economic development and a more important policy issue in many countries.

First, the private, market-based investment process—underpinned by good corporate governance—is much more important for most economies than it used to be. Privatization has raised corporate governance issues in sectors that were previously in the hands of the state. Firms have gone to public markets to seek capital, and mutual societies and partnerships have converted themselves into listed corporations.

Second, due to technological progress, liberalization and opening up of financial markets, trade liberalization, and other structural reforms—notably, price deregulation and the removal of restrictions on products and ownership—the allocation of capital within and across countries among competing purposes has become more complex, as has monitoring the use of capital. This makes good governance more important but also more difficult.

Third, as a result of the increasing size of firms and the growing role of financial intermediaries, the mobilization of capital has become increasingly removed from the principal owner. The role of institutional investors is growing in many countries, with many economies moving away from pay-as-you-go retirement systems to (more) funded systems. This increased delegation of investment has raised the need for good corporate governance arrangements.

Fourth, deregulation and reform have reshaped the local and global financial landscape. Long-standing institutional corporate governance arrangements are being replaced with new institutional arrangements, but in the meantime, inconsistencies and gaps have emerged.

Fifth, international financial integration has increased, and trade and investment flows are increasing. This has led to many cross-border issues in corporate governance. Cross-border investment has been increasing, for example, resulting in meetings of corporate governance cultures that are at times uneasy.

The Link between Corporate Governance and Other Foundations of Development

The research on the role of corporate governance for economic development and well-being is best understood from the broader perspective of other foundations for development. Five elements of this broad literature—finance, the structure of the financial system, property rights, competition and real-factor markets, and ownership structure and group affiliation—are worth highlighting.

Finance

The importance of the financial system for growth and poverty reduction has been clearly established over the past decade. One demonstration is the link between finance and growth. Almost regardless of how financial development is measured, there is a cross-country association between it and the level of per capita GDP growth. Numerous pieces of evidence have been assembled over the past few years to indicate with reasonable robustness that the relation is a causal one, not merely the result of better-performing countries both having larger financial systems and growing faster. The relationship has been established at the level of countries, industrial sectors, and firms, and it has consistently survived a rigorous series of econometric probes [as documented in World Bank (2001). For an early review see Levine (1997); for a recent review see Levine (2005).]

Banking Systems and Market Finance

The development of banking systems and market finance spurs economic growth. Banks and securities markets are complementary in their functions, although markets naturally play a greater role for listed firms. More generally, research provides support for the functional view of finance—the view that it is not financial institutions or financial markets but the functions that they perform that matter. For any regression model of growth that is selected and adapted by adding various measures of stock market development relative to banking system development, the results are consistent: none of these measures of financial sector structure has any statistically significant impact on growth (see Demirgüç-Kunt and Levine 2001).[2] To function well, financial institutions and financial markets, in turn, require certain foundations, including good governance.

Legal Foundations

Legal foundations affect a variety of factors that lead to higher growth, including financial market development, external financing, and the quality of investment. Legal foundations include property rights that are clearly defined and enforced and other key regulations (disclosure, accounting, and financial sector regulation and supervision).

Comparative corporate governance research took off following work by La Porta and others (1997, 1998). These two pivotal papers emphasize the importance of law and legal enforcement on the governance of firms, the development of markets, and economic growth.

Following these papers, numerous studies have documented institutional differences relevant for financial markets and other aspects.[3] These papers have established that the development of a country's financial markets is affected by these institutional characteristics and that institutional characteristics can have direct effects on growth. Beck, Levine, and Loayza (2000), for example, document how the quality of a country's legal system not only influences its financial sector development but also has a separate, additional effect on economic growth. In a cross-country study at the sectoral level, Claessens and Laeven (2003) report that in weaker legal environments, firms not only obtain less financing but also invest less in intangible assets. Both the less-than-optimal financing and the investment patterns in turn affect the economic growth of a sector.

Competition and Real-Factor Markets

In addition to financial and capital markets, other factor markets need to function well to prevent corporate governance problems. These real-factor markets include all output and input markets, including labor, raw materials, intermediate products, energy, and distribution services. Firms subject to more discipline in the real-factor markets are more likely to adjust their operations and management to maximize value added. Corporate governance problems are therefore less severe when competition is already high in real-factor markets.

Competition for good corporate governance is important in financial markets, as well. The ability of insiders, for example, to mistreat minority shareholders consistently can depend on the degree of competition and protection. If small shareholders have little alternative but to invest in low-yielding assets, for example, controlling shareholders may be better able to provide a below-market return on minority equity. Surprisingly, while this view is well accepted and generally acknowledged (see Khemani and Leechor 2001), there is little empirical evidence that such a complementary relationship exists between corporate governance and competition.[4]

Ownership Structures and Group Affiliation

The nature of the corporate governance problems that countries face varies over time and across countries. One factor of importance is ownership structure, which defines the nature of principal-agent issues. Another factor is group affiliation, which is especially important in emerging markets. Of course, ownership and group affiliation structures can vary over time and be endogenous to country circumstances, including legal and other foundations (see Shleifer and Vishny 1997). As such, ownership and group affiliation structures both affect the legal and regulatory infrastructure necessary for good corporate governance and are affected by the existing legal and regulatory infrastructure.

Much of the corporate governance literature has focused on conflicts between managers and owners (Berle and Means 1932). But around the world, except in the United States and to some degree in the United Kingdom, insider-controlled or closely held firms are the norms (La Porta and others 1999). These can be family-owned firms or firms controlled by financial institutions. Families such as the Peugeots in France, the Quandts in Germany, and the Agnellis in Italy hold large blocks of shares in even the largest firms and effectively control them (Barca and Becht 2001; Franks and Mayer 2001; Faccio and Lang 2002). Wealthy, powerful families dominate the ownership of most corporations in emerging markets (Claessens, Djankov, and Lang 2000; Lins 2003). In other countries, such as Japan and to some extent Germany, financial institutions control large parts of the corporate sector (La Porta and others 1999; Claessens, Djankov, and Lang 2000; Faccio and Lang 2002). This control is frequently reinforced through pyramids and webs of shareholdings that allow families or financial institutions to use ownership of one firm to control many more. Even in Canada and the United States, family-owned firms are not uncommon (Morck, Stangeland, and Yeung 2000; Gadhoum, Lang, and Young 2003; Anderson and Reeb 2003).

A corporation's ownership structure affects the nature of the agency problems among shareholders and between managers and outside shareholders. When ownership is diffuse, as it typically is in the U.S. and U.K. corporations, agency problems stem from the conflicts of interests between outside shareholders and managers who own an insignificant amount of equity in the firm (Jensen and Meckling 1976). When ownership is concentrated to a degree that one owner (or a few owners acting in concert) has effective control of the firm, the nature of the agency problem shifts away from manager–shareholder conflicts. The controlling owner is often also the manager or can otherwise be assumed to be willing and be able to closely monitor and discipline management. Information asymmetries can also be assumed to be less of a problem, as a controlling owner can invest the resources necessary to acquire necessary information. Correspondingly, the principal-agent problems will be less likely to concern management versus owners and more likely to concern minority versus controlling shareholders. In these countries, protection of minority rights is more often the key. Countries in which insider-held firms dominate will have different requirements in terms of corporate governance framework from those in which widely held firms dominate.

Many countries have large financial and industrial conglomerates and groups. In some groups, a bank or other financial institution lies at the apex of the group, as insurance companies do in Japan (Prowse 1990) and banks do in Germany (Gorton and Schmidt 2000b). In others, and often in emerging markets, a financial institution lies within the group [Khanna and Palepu 2000; Claessens, Fan, and Lang (forthcoming) document groups in East Asian countries].

Such groups can have many benefits for the firm and its investors, such as enabling the use of internal factor markets, which can be valuable in case of missing or incomplete external (financial) markets. Particularly in emerging markets, group affiliation can be valuable for firms. Groups or conglomerates can also impose costs, however. They are often less transparent and have less clear management structures, creating the possibility of worse corporate governance, including expropriation of minority rights (Johnson, La Porta, and others 2000).

The existence of such problems and related corporate governance issues also depends on the overall competitive structure of the economy and the role of the state. In more developed, more market-based economies that are also more competitive, group affiliation is less common. As with ownership structures, the direction of causality is unclear. It may be that the prevalence of groups undermines the drive to develop external (financial) markets. Alternatively, poorly developed external markets may increase the benefits of internal markets.

How Does Corporate Governance Affect Growth and Development?

The literature identifies several related channels through which corporate governance affects growth and development:

- Increased access to external financing by firms, which can lead to greater investment, higher growth, and more employment creation.

- Lower cost of capital and associated higher firm valuation, which makes more investments attractive to investors and leads to growth and employment.
- Better operational performance, through better allocation of resources and better management, which creates wealth.
- Reduced risk of financial crises, a particularly important effect, as financial crises can impose large economic and social costs.
- Better relationships with all stakeholders, which helps improve social and labor relationships and areas such as environmental protection.

All these channels matter for growth, employment, poverty, and well-being more generally. Empirical evidence has documented these relationships at the level of the country, the sector, and the individual firm as well as from the investor perspective. While the evidence is plentiful and continuing to accumulate, many of these results are partial analyses and may not go beyond associations. Some of these studies suffer from endogeneity issues: some firms, markets, or countries that adopt better corporate governance may be more developed or perform better as a result, while others may have adopted better corporate governance because they were more developed. Missing variables can also be important. Some other factors may drive both better corporate governance and better development or performance, obscuring causality. [For discussions of the econometric problems raised by endogeneity and missing variables, see Himmelberg (2002) and Coles, Lemmons, and Meschke (2003).]

Increased Access to Financing

Financial and capital markets are better developed in countries with strong protection of property rights, as the law and finance literature demonstrates. In particular, better creditor rights and shareholder rights have been shown to be associated with deeper and more developed banking and capital markets. Figure 1 depicts the relationship between an index of creditor rights (adjusted for the extent to which the rule of law is enforced in the country) and the depth of the financial system (as measured by the ratio of private credit to GDP). The creditor rights index, developed by La Porta and others (1998), is the summation of four dummy variables, with 4 as the highest possible score.[5] The rule of law is a measure of the judicial efficiency and integrity of the legal environment, as reported by La Porta and others (1998). Countries are sorted into four quartiles, depending on where they rank on a scale based on the product of their creditor rights and on the efficiency of the judicial system. The better creditor rights are defined and enforced, the more willing lenders are to extend financing.

A similar relationship exists between the quality of shareholder protection and the development of countries' capital markets. Figure 2 depicts the relationship between an index of shareholder rights [the index of La Porta and others (1998),

Figure 1. The Better Creditor Rights are Defined and Enforced, the more Willing Lenders are to Extend Credit

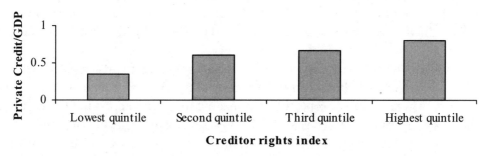

Note: The original rule of law data comes from the International Country Risk Guide. The data used here are the averages of the monthly index for April and October between 1982 and 1995.
Source: La Porta and others (1997).

Figure 2. The Stronger the Shareholder Protection, the Larger a Country's Stock Markets

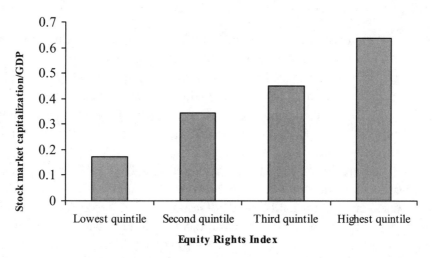

Source: La Porta and others (1997).

adjusted for the efficiency of the judicial system] and the size of the stock market (relative to GDP). The equity rights index is the summation of five dummy variables, with 5 as the highest possible score.[6] Countries are sorted into four quartiles, depending on where they rank on a scale based on the product of their equity rights and the efficiency of the judicial system.

The relationship between shareholder protection and capital market development is strong, with the market capitalization of the highest quartile of countries almost four times that of countries in the lowest quartile. The comparison between creditor rights and the development of private credit does not correct for other factors that affect financial sector development, such as inflation and macroeconomic performance. Yet almost all studies found that these results are robust to including a wide variety of control variables in the analysis (see Levine 2005).

In countries with better property rights, firms thus have greater access to financing. As a consequence, firms can be expected to invest more and grow faster. The effects on growth of better property rights leading to greater access to financing can be large. For example, countries in the third quartile of financial development enjoy 1.0–1.5 extra percentage points of GDP growth a year compared with countries in the first quartile (Rajan and Zingales 1998). There is also evidence that under conditions of poor corporate governance (and underdeveloped financial and legal systems and higher corruption), the growth rate of the smallest firms is the most adversely affected, and fewer new firms, particularly small firms, start up (Beck, Demirgüç-Kunt, and Maksimovic 2005).

Higher Firm Valuation

The quality of the corporate governance framework affects not only access to and the amount of external financing but also the cost of capital and firm valuation. Outsiders are less willing to provide financing and more likely to charge higher rates if they are less assured that they will earn an adequate rate of return (Morck, Shleifer, and Vishny 1988). Conflicts between small and large controlling shareholders are greater in weaker corporate governance settings, implying that smaller investors receive lower rates of return.

There is clear empirical evidence for these effects. The cost of capital has been shown to be higher and valuation to be lower in countries with weaker property rights (La Porta and others 2000, 2002; Claessens and others 2002). Investors also seem to discount their valuation of firms and countries with worse corporate governance (Doidge, Karolyi, and Stulz 2004; McKinsey and Company 2002). Furthermore, in countries with weaker property rights, controlling shareholders obtain a fraction of the value of the firm that exceeds their direct ownership stake, at the expense of minority shareholders.

Weak corporate governance appears to be associated with higher costs of capital, as examination of the prices paid in actual transactions for a block of shares that implies transferring control over the firm relative to the price of shares that do not and the equity rights index reveals (figure 3). The higher cost of capital, and the corresponding lower firm valuation, translates into economic costs for countries with worse corporate governance. Consequently, less attractive investments are bypassed.[7]

Figure 3. Weak Corporate Governance Translates into Higher Costs of Capital

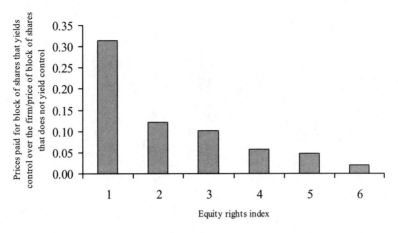

Source: Dyck and Zingales (2004) and Nenova (2003).

Better Operational Performance

Better corporate governance can add value by improving the performance of firms, through more efficient management, better asset allocation, better labor policies, or similar efficiency improvements. Evidence for the United States (Gompers, Ishii, and Metrick 2003), the Republic of Korea (Joh 2003), and elsewhere strongly suggests that at the firm level, better corporate governance leads to higher rates of return on equity, higher valuation, and higher profits and sales growth. This evidence is maintained when controlling for the fact that "better" firms may adopt better corporate governance and perform better due to other reasons. These and other firm-specific tests can nevertheless be criticized as suffering from endogeneity (see Himmelberg 2002). Across countries, there is also evidence that operational performance is higher in countries with better corporate governance, although the evidence is weaker (Wurgler 2000). In cross-country comparisons, there can also be a bias due to omitted variables. The issues of endogeneity and simultaneity of the various relationships also exist (it may be, for example, that better performing countries adopt better corporate governance and not that better corporate governance countries perform better).

Plotting accounting rates of return on assets for a sample of publicly listed firms using data from Worldscape against the equity rights index reveals that the relationship is much weaker than the relationship between the quality of the governance framework and access to financing and valuation (figure 4). Other factors evidently affect operational performance to mute this relationship. Many institutions and

Figure 4. Better Corporate Governance Translates into Somewhat Higher Returns on Assets

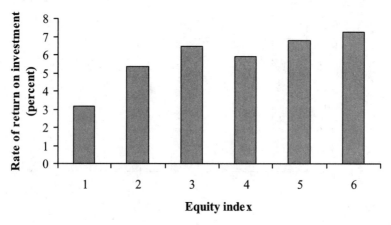

Note: The figure excludes Mexico and República Bolivariana de Venezuela, where rates of return were heavily influenced by inflation and currency movements.

Source: Data on returns are from Claessens, Djankov, and Nenova (2001) and cover 1996–99. The index on equity rights is from La Porta and others (1998).

factors influence a firm's management and performance. Firms in developing countries may face better growth opportunities, thus reporting higher profits, although they may have worse corporate governance. There may also be a reporting bias. Firms in environments with worse corporate governance may be more likely to overstate their accounting profits.

The limited relationship between operational performance and corporate governance measures at the country level may also reflect the fact that corporate governance in most countries does not concern a conflict between management and owners, leading to inefficient firm operation and low rates on assets. Rather, as most firms are closely held or controlled by insiders, corporate governance concerns conflicts between controlling shareholders and minority shareholders, leading to lower valuation and reduced access to external financing.

This interpretation is supported by comparing the rate of return on investment with the cost of capital for different corporate governance frameworks (figure 5). Plotting the rates of return on investment for a sample of some 19,000 publicly listed firms from a variety of countries against the equity rights index shows that firms in many countries do not earn the cost of capital required by shareholders; only in countries with the best corporate governance does the rate of return on investment exceed the cost of capital. The relationship derives, however, largely from the higher cost of capital, that is, the lower valuation of firms in weak corporate governance countries.

Figure 5. Higher equity rights translate into higher returns on investment relative to the cost of capital

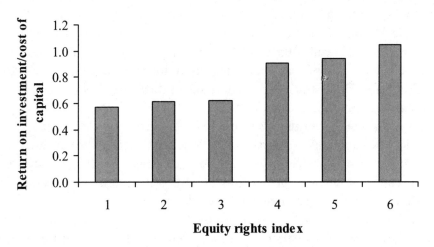

Note: Figure depicts the marginal rates of return on new investment adjusted for the cost of capital calculated using Tobin's Q model.

Source: Data on returns come from Gugler, Mueller, and Yurtoglu (2004), who use data from Worldscope. The index on equity rights is from La Porta and others (1998).

Reduced Risk of Financial Crises

The quality of corporate governance can also affect firms' behavior in times of economic shocks and actually contribute to the occurrence of financial distress, with economy-wide impacts. During the East Asian financial crisis, cumulative stock returns of firms in which managers had high levels of control rights but little direct ownership were 10–20 percentage points lower than those of other firms (Lemmon and Lins 2003). This finding suggests that corporate governance can play an important role in determining individual firms' behavior, in particular the incentives of insiders to expropriate minority shareholders during times of distress.

A study of the stock performance of listed companies in Indonesia, the Republic of Korea, Malaysia, the Philippines, and Thailand has found that performance is better in firms with higher accounting disclosure quality (proxied by the use of international auditors) and higher outside ownership concentration (Mitton 2002). There is also a similar evidence for the Republic of Korea on the importance of corporate governance for firm value during periods of financial turmoil (Baek, Kang, and Park 2004). This firm-level evidence is consistent with the view that corporate governance helps explain firm performance during a financial crisis.

Related work shows that hedging by firms is less common in countries with weak corporate governance frameworks (Lel 2003), and to the extent that it happens, it adds very little value (Alayannis, Lel, and Miller 2003), suggesting that in these environments, hedging is done more for the benefit of insiders than outsiders. There is also evidence that stock returns in emerging markets tend to be more positively skewed than in industrial countries (Bae, Lim, and Wei 2003). This can be attributed to the fact that managers have more discretion in emerging markets to withhold bad information or that firms share risks in these markets among themselves rather than through financial markets.

Country-level evidence suggests that weak legal institutions for corporate governance were key factors in exacerbating the stock market declines during the 1997 East Asian financial crisis (Johnson, Boone, and others 2000). In countries with weaker investor protection, net capital inflows were more sensitive to negative events that adversely affect investors' confidence. In such countries, the risk of expropriation increased during bad times, as the expected return of investment was lower, and the country was therefore more likely to witness collapses in currency and stock prices. Johnson, Boone, and others (2000) found a relationship between the efficiency of the judicial system and currency depreciation between the end of 1996 and the beginning of 1999, that is, during the East Asian and global financial crises.[8] More generally, a well-functioning financial and legal system can help reduce financial volatility.

The view that poor corporate governance of individual firms can have economy-wide effects is not limited to developing countries. Recently, the argument has been made that in industrial countries, corporate collapses (Enron), undue profit boosting (WorldCom), managerial corporate looting (Tyco), audit fraud (Arthur Andersen), and inflated reports of stock performance (by supposedly independent investment analysts) have led to crises of confidence among investors, leading to declines in stock market valuation and other economy-wide effects, including some slowdowns in economic growth. While this evidence is anecdotal, and weaker corporate governance has not triggered financial crises in these countries, it is clear that corporate governance deficiencies have started to carry a discount, for particular firms or markets as a whole, even in developed countries. Poor corporate governance practices can thus impose a negative externality on the economy as a whole in any country.

More generally, poor corporate governance can affect the functioning of a country's financial markets. One channel through which it can do so is by increasing financial volatility. When information is poorly protected—due to a lack of transparency and the fact that insiders know more about firms' activities and prospects—investors and analysts may have neither the ability to analyze firms (because it is very costly to collect information) nor the incentive to do so (because insiders benefit regardless). In such a weak property rights environment, inside investors with private information, including analysts, may, for example, trade on information before it is disclosed to the public. There is evidence that the lack of transparency associated with weaker corporate governance leads to more synchronous stock price movements, limiting the price discovery role of the stock markets (Morck, Young, and Yu 2000). A study of stock prices within a common trading mechanism and currency (the Hong Kong Stock Exchange) found that stocks from environments with less investor protection (China based) trade at higher bid-ask spreads and exhibit thinner depths than more protected (Hong Kong-based) stocks (Brockman and Chung 2003). Evidence on Canada suggests that ownership structures indicating potential corporate governance problems also affect the size of bid-ask spreads (Attig, Gadhoum, and Lang 2003).

Another area in which corporate governance affects firms and their valuation is mergers and acquisitions. During the 1990s, the volume of merger and acquisition activity and the premiums paid for such activity were significantly larger in countries with better investor protection (Rossi and Volpin 2003). This indicates that an active market for mergers and acquisitions—an important component of a corporate governance regime—arises only in countries with good investor protection. The analysis also shows that in cross-border deals, the acquirers are typically from countries with better investor protection than the targets. This suggests that cross-border transactions play a governance role by improving the degree of investor protection within target firms. It further suggests that cross-border transactions aid in the convergence of corporate governance systems.

Better Relations with Other Stakeholders

In addition to the principal owner and management, public and private corporations must deal with many other stakeholders, including banks, bondholders, labor, and local and national governments. Each of these groups monitors, disciplines, motivates, and affects management and the firm in various ways. They do so in exchange for some control and cash-flow rights, which relate to each stakeholder's comparative advantage, legal forms of influence, and form of contracts.

Commercial banks, for example, have more inside knowledge, as they typically have a continuing relationship with the firm. The formal influence of commercial banks may derive from the covenants banks impose on the firm (for example, in terms of dividend policies or requirements for approval of large investments, mergers and acquisitions, and other large undertakings). Bondholders may also have such covenants or even specific collateral. Furthermore, lenders have legal rights of a state-contingent nature. In case of financial distress, they acquire control rights; in case of bankruptcy, they may obtain ownership rights, as defined by the country's laws.[9] Debt and debt structure can be important disciplining factors, as they can limit free cash flow and thereby reduce private benefits. Trade finance can play a special role, as it will be a short-maturity claim, with perhaps some specific collateral.

Suppliers can have particular insights into the operation of the firm, as they are more aware of the economic and financial prospects of the industry.

Labor has a number of rights and claims. As with other input factors, an outside market for employment exists, which puts pressure on firms to provide not only financially attractive but also socially attractive opportunities. Labor laws define many of the relationships between corporations and labor, which may have some corporate governance aspects. The rights of employees in firm affairs can be formally defined, as they are in France, Germany, and The Netherlands, where large companies are required to give labor some seats on the board (the co-determination model).[10] Employees, of course, voice their opinion on firm management more generally. The market for senior management, in which poorly performing CEOs and other senior managers get fired, exerts some discipline on poor performance.

Two forms of behavior can be distinguished in corporate governance issues related to other stakeholders—stakeholder management and participation in social issues. For the first category, the firm has no choice but to behave "responsibly" toward stakeholders: stakeholders are input factors without which the firm cannot operate, and they face alternative opportunities if the firm does not treat them well (labor can typically work elsewhere). Acting responsibly toward stakeholders is thus necessary. Acting responsibly is also most likely to be beneficial to the firm, financially and otherwise.

Acting responsibly may also benefit the firm's shareholders and other stakeholders. For example, a firm with a good relationship with its workers will probably find it easier to attract external financing. Collectively, a high degree of corporate responsibility can ensure good relationships with all the firm's stakeholders, thereby improving the firm's overall financial performance. Of course, the effects depend on information and reputation; knowing which firms behave more responsibly to stakeholders will not always be easy.

Whether participation in social issues is also related to good firm performance is less clear. Involvement in some social issues carries costs. Costs can be direct, as when expenditures for charitable donations or environmental protection increase. Costs can also be indirect, as when the firm becomes less flexible and operates less efficiently.

Socially responsible behavior could be considered "bad" corporate governance, as it negatively affects performance. (If government regulations require certain behavior, such as safeguarding the environment, the firm has no choice, although the country does.)

The general argument has been that these forms of social corporate responsibility can still pay, that is, they can be good business for all and go hand-in-hand with good corporate governance. So while there may be little direct business justification for respecting the environment or donating to social charity, for example, such actions can create positive externalities in the form of better relationships with other stakeholders. The willingness, for example, of many firms to adopt high international standards, such as ISO 9000, that go beyond the narrow interest of production and sales suggests that there are perceived positive effects at the firm level.

Few empirical studies have documented these effects. The general evidence is either mixed or shows no relationship between corporate social responsibility and financial performance. At the country level, more developed countries tend to have both better corporate governance and rules requiring more socially responsible behavior of corporations. There is also some evidence, however, that government-forced forms of stakeholdership may be less advantageous financially. One study of Germany finds that workers' co-determination reduced market-to-book values and return on equity (Gorton and Schmidt 2000a).

As with many other corporate governance studies, the problem is in part the endogeneity of the relationships. At the firm level, does good corporate performance beget better social corporate responsibility, or does better social corporate responsibility lead to better performance? Firms that adopt ISO standards, for example, may well have performed better than firms that did not even before adopting such standards. At the country level, a higher level of development may well allow and create pressures for greater social responsibility, while at the same time improving corporate governance.

Reform of Corporate Governance

The analysis so far suggests that better corporate governance generally pays for firms, markets, and countries. The question then arises why firms, markets, and countries do not adjust and voluntarily adopt better corporate governance measures. The answer is that firms, markets, and countries do adjust to some extent but that these steps fail to provide the full impact, work only imperfectly, and involve considerable costs. The main reasons for lack of sufficient reforms are entrenched owners and managers at the firm level and political economy factors at the level of markets and countries. Both issues are considered below.

The Role of Entrenched Owners and Managers

Evidence shows that firms adapt to weaker environments by adopting voluntary corporate governance measures. A firm may adjust its ownership structure, for example, by having more secondary, large blockholders, who can serve as effective monitors of the primary controlling shareholders. This may convince minority shareholders of the firm's willingness to respect their rights. A firm may adjust its dividend behavior if it has been having difficulty convincing shareholders that it will reinvest properly and for their benefit. These voluntary mechanisms can include hiring more reputable auditors. Since auditors have some reputation at stake, they may agree to conduct an audit only if the firm is making sufficient efforts to enhance its corporate governance. The more reputable the auditor, the more the firm needs to improve its corporate governance. A firm can also issue capital or list its shares abroad, thereby subjecting itself to a higher level of corporate governance and disclosure.

Empirical evidence shows that these mechanisms can add value and are appreciated by investors in a variety of countries. A study of a sample of U.S. firms finds that the more the firms adopt voluntary corporate governance mechanisms, the higher their valuation and lower their cost of capital (Gompers, Ishii, and Metrick 2003). Similar evidence exists for the Republic of Korea (Black, Jang, and Kim 2002), the Russian Federation (Black 2001), and the top 300 European firms (Bauer and Guenster 2003).[11] Gompers, Ishii, and Metrick (2003) report that these firms have higher profitability and sales growth and that they lower their capital expenditures and acquisitions to levels that are presumably more efficient.

Evidence also suggests that the voluntary corporate governance adopted by firms matters more in weak corporate governance environments. Two studies compare indexes of firm-specific corporate governance measures with countries' corporate governance indexes to analyze the effects on firm valuation and firm performance (Klapper and Love 2005; Durnev and Kim 2005). They found that the firm-level corporate governance matters more to firm value in countries with weaker investor protection. Markets can adapt as well, partly in response to competition, as listing and trading migrate to competing exchanges, for example. While there can be races to the bottom, with firms and markets seeking lower standards, markets can and will set their own, higher corporate governance standards. One example is the Novo Mercado in Brazil, which has different levels of corporate governance standards, all higher than the main stock exchange, among which firms can choose. The system is backed by private arbitration measures to settle corporate governance disputes. Efforts like these can help corporations improve corporate governance at low(er) costs, as they can list locally.

There is evidence, however, that these alternative corporate governance mechanisms, in addition to being costly, have their limits. In a context of weak institutions and poor property rights, firm measures cannot and do not fully compensate for deficiencies. Klapper and Love (2005) and Durnev and Kim (2005) show that voluntary corporate governance adopted by firms only partially compensates for weak corporate governance environments.

There are also elements of self-selection, with weaker firms choosing to list in weaker environments. Competition between stock exchanges takes many forms, including not only listing standards but also the direct cost of trading. This suggests that firms consider several dimensions in selecting where to list. Coffee (1999, 2001) argues that family-owned firms prefer to list in weak corporate governance environments (with perhaps higher trading costs). These markets have little incentives to improve their corporate governance standards. By contrast (large) firms with diversified ownership structures prefer to list in international markets. There are many other reasons why firms do not adjust their corporate governance or list in the environment optimal from a cost of capital point of view, including entrenched owners and employees.

The Role of Political Economy Factors

Countries do not always reform their corporate governance frameworks to achieve the best possible outcomes. In some sense, this is shown by the pervasive importance of the origin of the legal system in a particular country. Whether a country started with a certain legal system or acquired it as a result of colonization has a systematic impact on its legal system, the performance of its judicial system, the regulation of labor markets, entry by new firms, the development of its financial sector, state ownership, and other important characteristics (Djankov and others 2003). Evidently, countries do not adjust easily and move to better standards to fit their own circumstances and meet their own needs. Partly this is because reforms are multifaceted and require a mixture of legal, regulatory, and market measures, making progress difficult and slow. Efforts may have to be coordinated among many constituents, including foreign parties. Legal and regulatory changes must take into account enforcement capacity, often a binding constraint. While markets face competition and can adapt themselves, they must operate within the limits of a country's legal framework.

The Novo Mercado in Brazil is a notable exception in which the local market has attempted to improve corporate governance standards using voluntary mechanisms. But it needs to rely on mechanisms such as arbitration to settle corporate governance disputes as an alternative to the poorly functioning judicial system in Brazil. Experiments with self-regulation in corporate governance, such as those in The Netherlands, have often not been successful.[12] The ability of corporations to borrow the framework from other jurisdictions by listing or raising capital abroad, or even incorporating, is limited to the extent that some local enforcement of rules is needed, particularly concerning protection of minority rights (see Siegel 2005 for the case of Mexico).

Corporate governance reforms involve changes in control and power structures. As such, they can depend on ownership structures. In parts of East Asia, for instance, where a small number of families hold a large share of corporate sector wealth, the degree to which corporate governance standards have been enhanced has been negatively correlated with the share of corporate sector wealth held by those families (Claessens, Djankov, and Lang 1999).

Ownership concentration and institutional development are inversely correlated in a sample of East Asian countries (figure 6). Causality is unclear, however, as weak

Figure 6. The concentration of wealth and institutional reform are inversely correlated in East Asia

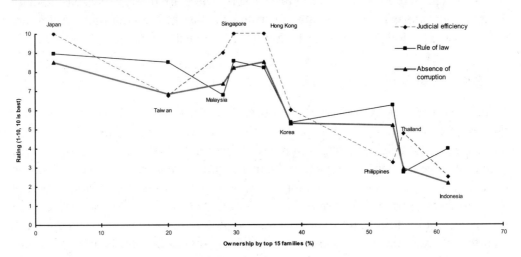

Note: Figure depicts indexes of the quality of the institutional environment, from 1 to 10 with 10 best, that assess the efficiency and integrity of the legal environment and the absence of corruption as they affect business, particularly foreign firms, against the corporate sector ownership by the top 15 families, expressed as a percentage of total market capitalization.

Source: Claessens, Djankov, and Lang (1999).

corporate governance standards could have led to more concentrated corporate sector wealth. Conversely, a higher concentration of wealth could have impeded improvements in corporate governance. In Indonesia, for example, there are many direct relationships between the government and the corporate sector. These considerations notwithstanding, the correlation does suggest that ownership structures can impede significant corporate governance reform.

Morck, Wolfenzohn, and Yeung (2004) review the literature on how, at the economy level, extensive control of corporate assets by a few families can distort capital allocation and reduce the rate of innovation. They argue that families appear to influence the development of both public policy, such as property rights protection and enforcement, and institutions such as capital markets. They show that per capita GDP growth is faster in countries in which the ratio of self-made billionaire wealth to GDP is larger but that per capita GDP growth is slower in countries in which inherited billionaire wealth represents a larger share of GDP. Morck and Yeung (2004) show that there is a strong correlation between the degree of family control and measures of entry barriers, judicial system inefficiencies, and political and tax system corruption. They also found that the separation of ownership and control—through pyramids, differential voting, and other arrangements—contributes to inefficiencies.

The World Bank Research Observer, vol. 21, no. 1 (Spring 2006)

The samples studied are often too small to make any statistical inference, and the evidence is based too much on cross-country evidence to make strong causal statements. Nevertheless, it does suggest that wealth structures may need to change to bring about significant institutional reform. This can happen through legal changes over time or as a result of direct interventions, such as privatization and nationalization, as during financial crises.

Reforms can be impeded by a lack of understanding, which can be affected by political economy factors. Some of these, such as tight control over the media, may be directly related to ownership structures. And it is not just ownership that matters. The theoretical literature on the political economy of finance has highlighted a likely coincidence of interests between large shareholders (inside capital) and workers in the formal sector (inside labor) to the detriment of more dispersed interests, such as outside investors or consumers (Pagano and Volpin 2005; Perotti and von Thadden 2003). The intuition is that an implicit alliance aimed at limiting external challenges to local producers generates rents that can be shared between inside capital and inside labor. This alliance can grant extensive control benefits to large shareholders at the cost of outside investors, supported by higher rents for inside labor. It creates, however, serious rigidities, which undermine promoting the most efficient producers; attracting external financial resources to fund entry, renewal, and growth; and reallocating resources across sectors and producers.

The relationships between institutional features and countries' more permanent characteristics, including culture, history, and physical endowments, have not been widely researched. Institutional characteristics (such as the risk of expropriation of private property) can be long lasting and relate to a country's physical endowments (as Acemoglu and others 2003 show for a cross-section of countries). Both the origin of a country's legal systems and its initial endowments are important determinants of the degree of private property rights protection (Pistor 2000; Beck, Demirgüç-Kunt, and Levine 2003). The role of culture and openness in finance, including in corporate governance, is also important (Stulz and Williamson 2003).

More generally, the dynamic aspects of corporate governance reform are not yet well understood. Rajan and Zingales (2003a) study the underlying political economy factors that may drive changes in the legal frameworks over time. They highlight the fact that many European countries had more developed capital markets in 1913 than for a long period after World War II. In 1913, capital markets in many of these countries were more developed than in the United States. A review of ownership structures at the end of the nineteenth century in the United Kingdom shows that most firms there had widely dispersed ownership before they were floated on the stock exchanges (Franks, Mayer, and Rossi 2003). In Italy, the ownership structures were more diffuse in 1940 than in the 1980s (Aganin and Volpin 2003). These three studies cast some doubt on the view that stock market development and ownership concentration are monotonically related to investor protection.

These studies identify the issue, but they do not clarify the channels through which institutional features alter financial markets and corporate governance over time or show how institutional features change. They represent the beginning of a research agenda (see also Rajan and Zingales 2003b). A more general review of the "new comparative economics" literature can be found in Djankov and others (2003), who highlight the many areas about which little is known.[13]

Conclusions and Areas for Future Research

The importance of corporate governance for access to financing, the cost of capital, valuation, and performance has been documented at the firm level in a number of countries. Better corporate governance leads to higher returns on equity and greater efficiency. Across countries, the important role of institutions aimed at contractual and legal enforcement, including corporate governance, has been underscored by the law and finance literature. At the country level, various papers have documented a number of differences in institutional features. Across countries, the relationships between institutional features and development of financial markets, relative corporate sector valuations, efficiency of investment allocation, and economic growth have been shown. Using firm-level data, researchers have documented relationships between countries' corporate governance frameworks on the one hand and performance, valuation, the cost of capital, and access to external financing on the other.

While the general importance of corporate governance has been established, knowledge is still weak in a number of areas:

- *Corporate governance of banks.* Corporate governance of banks has been shown to be different from that of corporations, but the ways in which it differs (other than the important role of prudential regulations) are not clear. Clarifying this issue is important, because banks are important providers of external financing, especially for small- and medium-size firms. In addition, in many countries, banks play important corporate governance roles, as they are direct investors themselves or act as agents for other investors. Creditors, including banks, can see their credit claim change into an ownership stake when a firm runs into bankruptcy or financial distress.
- *Role of institutional investors.* The importance of institutional investors is increasing throughout the world, and their role in the corporate governance of firms is consequently becoming more important. But the role of institutional investors in corporate governance is not obvious. In many countries, institutional investors have been assigned little role in corporate governance, for fear of endangering their fiduciary obligations. The governance of institutional investors

themselves is also an issue, as they will not exercise good corporate governance without being governed themselves properly. Moreover, the form through which more activism of institutional investors can be achieved is not clear, as they typically hold small stakes in individual firms. Some form of coordination is thus necessary, but too much coordination can be harmful, as the financial institutions start to collude and political economy factors start to play a role.

- *Enforcement.* How can enforcement be improved in weak environments? How can a better enforcement environment be engineered? More generally, what factors determine the degree to which the private sector can solve enforcement problems on it own, and what determines the need for public sector involvement in enforcement?

- *State-owned firms.* What is the role of commercialization in state-owned enterprises? Are there special corporate governance issues in cooperatively owned firms? How do privatization and corporate governance frameworks interact? Are some forms of privatization more attractive in weak corporate governance settings? What are the dynamic relationships between corporate governance changes and changes in the degree of state-ownership of commercial enterprises?

- *Family-owned firms.* Family-owned firms predominate in many sectors and economies. They raise a set of issues related to liquidity, growth, and transition to a more widely held corporation, as well as issues related to internal management, such as intra-familial disagreements, disputes about succession, and exploitation of family members. Where family-owned firms dominate, as in many emerging markets, they raise system-wide corporate governance issues.

- *Best practice in relation to other stakeholders.* Little empirical research has been conducted on the relationships between corporate governance and social corporate responsibility. The research that has been conducted has been on firms in developed countries.

- *Impact on poverty alleviation.* Although the general importance of property rights for poverty alleviation has been established (De Soto 1989, North 1990), the channels through which improved corporate governance can help the poor have not been documented. This is in part because much of the corporate governance research has studied listed firms. Much of the job creation in developing countries and emerging markets comes from small- and medium-size enterprises, which face different corporate governance issues.

- *Dynamic aspects of institutional change.* Little is known about the dynamic aspects of institutional change, whether change occurs in a more evolutionary way during normal times or more abruptly during times of financial or political crises.

Enhancing corporate governance will remain very much a local effort. Country-specific circumstances and institutional features mean that global findings do not necessarily apply directly to every country or situation. Local data need to be used to make a convincing case for change. Local capacity is needed to identify the relevant issues and make use of political opportunities for legal and regulatory reform. Corporate governance reform thus depends on local capacity in terms of data, people, and other resources.

Notes

Stijn Claessens is professor of international finance policy at the University of Amsterdam, senior adviser to the Financial Sector Vice-Presidency of the World Bank, and a fellow of the Centre for Economic Policy Research; his e-mail address is sclaessens@worldbank.org. This article is based on a presentation to the Global Corporate Governance Forum donors meeting held in The Hague, March 13, 2003. The author would like to thank the participants for their comments, and the editors and both reviewers for their comments.

1. The first broad survey of corporate governance was by Shleifer and Vishny (1997). Several surveys followed, including Becht, Bolton and Röell (2003), Denis and McConnell (2003), Holderness (2003), and Holmstrom and Kaplan (2001). Tirole (2001) provides an analytical review. Claessens and Fan (2002) survey the literature on Asia corporate governance.

2. There appears to be no effect on the sectoral composition of growth or on the proportion of firms growing more rapidly that could be financed from internal resources; even bank profitability does not appear to be affected (World Bank 2001). This is the case regardless of whether the ratio employed relates to the volume of assets (bank deposits, stock market capitalization) or to efficiency (net interest margin, stock turnover).

3. All these applications are important, although not novel. Coase (1937, 1960), Alchian (1965), Demsetz (1964), Demsetz and Lehn (1985), Cheung (1970, 1983), North (1981, 1990), and subsequent research on institutions have long stressed the interaction between property rights and institutional arrangements in shaping economic behavior. The work of La Porta and others (1997, 1998), however, provided the tools with which to compare institutional frameworks across countries and to study the effects in a number of dimensions, including how a country's legal framework affects firms' external financing and investment. Since then, many other studies have documented institutional differences.

4. In a paper on Poland, Grosfeld and Tressel (2002) found that competition had a positive effect on firms with good corporate governance but no significant effects on firms with bad corporate governance.

5. The dummy variables describe the legal system for creditors in the country. The dummies are as follows: restrictive reorganization, equal to 1 if the time table for rendering a judgment during the restructuring phase is less than 90 days and 0 otherwise; mandatory management turnover (in reorganization), equal to 1 if incumbent management does not stay during a restructuring or bankruptcy and 0 otherwise; no automatic stay, equal to 1 if there is no automatic stay on assets (that is, no moratorium on payments) and 0 otherwise; secured creditors priority, equal to 1 if secured creditors have the highest priority in payment and 0 otherwise. See also Claessens and Klapper (2005).

6. The equity rights index includes the following dummy variables, with each dummy equal to 1 if the provision is present in the law and 0 otherwise: the country allows shareholders to mail their proxy vote; shareholders are not required to deposit their shares before the general shareholders' meeting; cumulative voting is allowed; an oppressed minorities mechanism is in place; the minimum percentage of share capital that entitles a shareholder to call an extraordinary shareholders' meeting is less than or equal to 10 percent.

7. A number of country studies corroborate the cross-country evidence on the costs of poor corporate governance. Johnson, Boone, and others (2000), Bae, Kang, and Kim (2002), and Bertrand,

Mehta, and Mullainathan (2002) analyze the siphoning-off of funds by controlling shareholders in the Czech Republic, the Republic of Korea, and India, respectively. The misuse by controlling shareholders translates into higher cost of capital.

8. This may have been a specific phenomenon experienced only in this time period, when many emerging markets were faced with financial stress. It is not observed in other periods. The perverse effects of weak corporate governance may thus depend on the state of the economy.

9. Note the large differences between countries in this respect. In the United States, for example, banks are limited in intervening in corporations' operations, as they can be deemed to be acting in the role of a shareholder. They therefore assume the position of a junior claimholder in case of a bankruptcy (the doctrine of equitable subordination). This greatly limits the incentives of U.S. banks to get involved in corporate governance issues, as such involvement could lower their credit claim standing. Other countries allow banks a greater role in corporate governance.

10. Employee ownership is, of course, the most direct way in which labor can have a stake in a firm. Kruse and Blasi (1995, p. 1) summarize the empirical evidence on the effects of employee ownership for U.S. firms. They found that "while few studies individually find clear links between employee ownership and firm performance, meta-analyses favor an overall positive association with performance for employee stock ownership plans (ESOPs) and for several cooperative features."

11. For the top 300 European firms, a strategy of overweighting companies with good corporate governance and underweighting those with bad corporate governance would have yielded an annual excess return of 2.97 percent (Bauer and Guenster 2003).

12. Suggestions by The Netherlands' corporate governance reform committee in 1997 stressed self-enforcement through market forces to implement and enforce its recommendations. A review of progress in 2003 (Peters Report 2003), however, showed that this model had not worked and that more legal changes would be needed to improve corporate governance. Earlier empirical work (De Jong and others 2001) anticipated this effect, documenting the mild market response when the recommendations were announced.

13. In a study investigating the effects of institutional factors more generally, Glaeser and others (2004) found that many of the institutional variables used to establish the proposition that institutions cause growth are either not appropriate or are not robust empirically.

References

Acemoglu, D., S. Johnson, J. Robinson, and Y. Thaicharoen. 2003. "Institutional Causes, Macroeconomic Symptoms: Volatility, Crises and Growth." *Journal of Monetary Economics* (Netherlands) 50(1):49–131.

Aganin, Alexander, and Paolo Volpin. 2003. "History of Corporate Ownership in Italy." Finance Working Paper 17/2003. European Corporate Governance Institute, Brussels.

Alayannis, George, Ugur Lel, and Darius Miller. 2003. "Corporate Governance and the Hedging Premium." Darden Business School, University of Virginia, Charlottesville.

Alchian, A. A. 1965. "Some Economics of Property Rights." *Il Politico* 30:816–29.

Anderson, Ronald C., and David M. Reeb. 2003. "Founding-Family Ownership and Firm Performance: Evidence from the S&P 500." *Journal of Finance* 58(3):1301–28.

Attig, Najah, Yoser Gadhoum, and Larry H. P. Lang. 2003. "Bid-Ask Spread, Asymmetric Information and Ultimate Ownership." Chinese University of Hong Kong, Department of Finance.

Bae, K. H., J. K. Kang, and J. M. Kim. 2002. "Tunneling or Value Addition? Evidence from Mergers by Korean Business Groups." *Journal of Finance* 57(6):2695–740.

Bae, K. H., Chanwoo Lim, and K. C. John Wei. 2003. "Corporate Governance and Conditional Skewness in World's Stock Markets." Hong Kong University of Science and Technology, Department of Finance.

Baek, Jae-Seung, Jun- Koo Kang, and Kyung Suh Park. 2004. "Corporate Governance and Firm Value: Evidence from the Korean Financial Crisis." *Journal of Financial Economics* 71(2):265–313.

Barca, Fabrizio, and Marco Becht, eds. 2001. *The Control of Corporate Europe*. Oxford: Oxford University Press.

Bauer, Rob, and Nadja Guenster. 2003. "Good Corporate Governance Pays Off! Well-Governed Companies Perform Better on the Stock Market." Algemeen Burgelijk Pensioenfonds, Heerlen, Netherlands. [http://www.deminorrating.com].

Becht, Marco, Patrick Bolton, and Alisa Roell. 2003. "Corporate Governance and Control." In George Constantinides, Milton Harris, and René Stulz, eds, *Handbook of the Economics of Finance*. Amsterdam: North-Holland.

Beck, Thorsten, Ross Levine, and Norman Loayza. 2000. "Finance and the Sources of Growth." *Journal of Financial Economics* 58(1–2):261–300.

Beck, Thorsten, Asli Demirgüç-Kunt, and Ross Levine. 2003. "Law, Endowments, and Finance." *Journal of Financial Economics* 70(2):137–81.

Beck, Thorsten, Asli Demirgüç-Kunt, and Vojislav Maksimovic. 2005. "Financial and Legal Constraints to Firm Growth: Does Size Matter?" *Journal of Finance* 60(1):137–77.

Berle, A. A., and G. Means. 1932. *The Modern Corporation and Private Property*. New York: Macmillan.

Bertrand, M., P. Mehta, and S. Mullainathan. 2002. "Ferreting Out Tunneling: An Application to Indian Business Groups." *Quarterly Journal of Economics* 117(1):121–48.

Black, Bernard. 2001. "The Corporate Governance Behavior and Market Value of Russian Firms." *Emerging Markets Review* 2(2):89–108.

Black, Bernard S., H. Jang, and W. Kim. 2002. "Does Corporate Governance Matter? Evidence from the Korean Market." Working Paper, Stanford Law School, Stanford, Calif., and Korea University and KDI School of Public Policy and Management, Seoul.

Bodie, Zvi, and Robert Merton. 1995. "A Conceptual Framework of Analyzing the Financial Environment." In Dwight B Crane, Zvi Bodie, Kenneth A. Froot, Andre F. Perold, and Robert C. Merton, eds, *The Global Financial System: A Functional Perspective*. Boston: Harvard Business School Press.

Brockman, Paul, and Dennis Y. Chung. 2003. "Investor Protection and Firm Liquidity." *Journal of Finance* 58(2):921–37.

Cadbury Committee (Committee on the Financial Aspects of Corporate Governance). 1992. "The Report of the Committee on the Financial Aspects of Corporate Governance." London.

Cheung, S. N. S. 1970. "The Structure of a Contract and the Theory of Nonexclusive Resource." *Journal of Law and Economics* 13(54):49–70.

———. 1983. "The Contractual Nature of the Firm." *Journal of Law and Economics* 26(1):1–21.

Claessens, Stijn, Simeon Djankov, and Larry H. P. Lang. 1999. "Who Controls East Asian Corporations and the Implications for Legal Reform." Public Policy of the Private Sector Viewpoint Note 195, World Bank, Private Sector Development Department, Washington, D.C.

———. 2000. "The Separation of Ownership and Control in East Asian Corporations." *Journal of Financial Economics* 58(1–2):81–112.

Claessens, Stijn, Simeon Djankov, and Tatiana Nenova. 2001. "Corporate Risk around the World." In Reuven Glick, Ramon Moreno, and Mark Spiegel, eds, *Financial Crises in Emerging Markets*. Cambridge: Cambridge University Press.

Claessens, Stijn, and Joseph P. H. Fan. 2002. "Corporate Governance in Asia: A Survey." *International Review of Finance* 3(2):105–29.

Claessens, Stijn, Simeon Djankov, Joseph P. H. Fan, and Larry H. P. Lang. 2002. "Disentangling the Incentive and Entrenchment Effects of Large Shareholdings." *Journal of Finance* 57(6):2741–71.

Claessens, Stijn, and Luc Laeven. 2003. "Financial Development, Property Rights, and Growth." *Journal of Finance* 58(6):2401–36.

Claessens, Stijn, and L. Klapper. 2005. "Bankruptcy around the World: Explaining Its Relative Use." *American Law and Economics Review* 7(1):253–83.

Claessens, Stijn, Joseph P. H. Fan, and Larry H. P. Lang. Forthcoming. "The Benefits and Costs of Group Affiliation: Evidence from East Asia." *Emerging Markets Review.*

Coase, Ronald C. 1937. "The Nature of the Firm." *Economica* 4(16):386–405.

———. 1960. "The Problem of Social Cost." *Journal of Law and Economics* 3(1):1–44.

Coffee, John C. 1999. "The Future as History: The Prospects for Global Convergence in Corporate Governance and its Implications." *Northwestern University Law Review* 93(3):641–708.

———. 2001. "Convergence and Its Critics: What Are the Preconditions to the Separation of Ownership and Control?" Columbia Law and Economics Working Paper 179, Columbia University, New York.

Coles, Jeffery L., Michael L., Lemmon, and J. Felix Meschke. 2003. "Structural Models and Endogeneity in Corporate Finance." Arizona State University, Department of Finance, Tempe.

De Jong, Abe, Douglas V. DeJong, Gerard Mertens, and Charles E. Wasley. 2001. "The Role of Self-Regulation in Corporate Governance: Evidence from the Netherlands." Simon School of Business Working Paper FR 00–20, University of Rochester, N.Y.

De Soto, Hernando. 1989. *The Other Path.* New York: Harper and Row.

Demirgüç-Kunt, Asli, and Ross Levine, eds. 2001. Financial Structure and Economic Growth: A Cross-Country Comparison of Banks, Markets, and Development. Cambridge, Mass.: MIT Press.

Demsetz, Harold. 1964. "The Exchange and Enforcement of Property Rights." *Journal of Law and Economics* 3(October): 11–26.

Demsetz, Harold, and K. Lehn. 1985. "The Structure of Corporate Ownership: Causes and Consequences." *Journal of Political Economy* 93(6):1155–77.

Denis, D. K., and J. J. McConnell. 2003. "International Corporate Governance." *Journal of Financial Quantitative Analysis* 38(1):1–27.

Djankov, Simeon, Edward L. Glaeser, Rafael La Porta, Florencio López-de-Silanes, and Andrei Shleifer. 2003. "The New Comparative Economics." *Journal of Comparative Economics* 31(4):595–619.

Doidge, C., A. Karolyi, and R. Stulz. 2004. "Why Are Foreign Firms Listed in the U.S. Worth More?" *Journal of Financial Economics* 71(2):205–38.

Durnev, A., and E. H. Kim. 2005. "To Steal or Not to Steal: Firm Attributes, Legal Environment, and Valuation." *Journal of Finance* 60(3):1461–93.

Dyck, Alexander, and Luigi Zingales. 2004. "Private Benefits of Control: An International Comparison." *Journal of Finance* 59(2):537–600.

Faccio, Mara, and Larry H. P. Lang. 2002. "The Ultimate Ownership of Western European Corporations." *Journal of Financial Economics* 65(3):365–95.

Franks, Julian, and Colin Mayer. 2001. "Ownership and Control of German Corporations." *Review of Financial Studies* 14(4):943–77.

Franks, Julian, Colin Mayer, and Stefano Rossi. 2003. "The Origination and Evolution of Ownership and Control." ECGI Finance Working Paper 09/2003, European Corporate Governance Institute, Brussels.

Gadhoum, Yoser, Larry H. P. Lang, and Leslie Young. 2003. "Who Controls US?" Chinese University of Hong Kong, Department of Finance.

Glaeser, Edward L., Rafael La Porta, Florencio Lopez-de-Silanes, and Andrei Shleifer. 2004. "Do Institutions Cause Growth?" *Journal of Economic Growth* 9(3):271–303.

Gompers, P. A., J. Ishii, and A. Metrick. 2003. "Corporate Governance and Equity Prices." *Quarterly Journal of Economics* 118(1):107–55.

Gorton, Gary, and F. A. Schmidt. 2000a. *Class Struggle inside the Firm: A Study of German Codetermination.* NBER Working Paper 7945. Cambridge, Mass.: National Bureau of Economic Research.

———. 2000b. "Universal Banking and the Performance of German Firms." *Journal of Financial Economics* 58(1–2):29–80.

Grosfeld, Irena, and Thierry Tressel. 2002. "Competition and Ownership Structure: Substitutes or Complements? Evidence from the Warsaw Stock Exchange." *Economics of Transition* 10(3):525–51.

Gugler, Klaus Peter, Dennis Mueller, and Burcin Yurtoglu. 2004. "Corporate Governance and Returns on Investment." *Journal of Law and Economics* 47(2):589–633.

Himmelberg, Charles P. R. 2002. "Measuring the Real Effects of Corporate Governance: A Note for the GCGF Research Meeting." Working Paper, Columbia University, Department of Economics, New York.

Holderness, Clifford. 2003. "A Survey of Blockholders and Corporate Control." *Economic Policy Review, Federal Reserve Bank of New York* 9(1):51–63.

Holmstrom, Bengt, and Steven N. Kaplan. 2001. "Corporate Governance and Merger Activity in the United States: Making Sense of the 1980s and 1990s." *Journal of Economic Perspectives* 15(Spring): 121–44.

Jensen, M. C., and W. H. Meckling, 1976. "Theory of the Firm: Managerial Behavior, Agency Costs and Ownership Structure." *Journal of Financial Economics* 3(4):305–60.

Joh, S. W. 2003. "Corporate Governance and Firm Profitability: Evidence from Korea before the Economic Crisis." *Journal of Financial Economics* 68(2):287–322.

Johnson, S., P. Boone, A. Breach, and E. Friedman. 2000. "Corporate Governance in the Asian Financial Crisis." *Journal of Financial Economics* 58(1–2):141–86.

Johnson, Simon, Rafael La Porta, Florencio Lopez-de-Silanes, and Andrei Shleifer. 2000. "Tunneling." *American Economic Review* 90(2) (*Papers and Proceedings*): 22–27.

Khanna, T., and K. Palepu. 2000. "Is Group Membership Profitable in Emerging Markets? An Analysis of Diversified Indian Business Groups." *Journal of Finance* 55(2):867–91.

Khemani, R. Shyam, and Chad Leechor. 2001. "Competition Boosts Corporate Governance." World Bank, Private Sector Development, Washington, D.C.

Klapper, L., and I. Love. 2005. "Corporate Governance, Investor Protection, and Performance in Emerging Markets." *Journal of Corporate Finance* 10(5):703–28.

Kruse, Douglas, and Joseph Blasi. 1995. *Employee Ownership, Employee Attitudes, and Firm Performance.* NBER Working Paper 5277. Cambridge, Mass.: National Bureau of Economic Research.

La Porta, Rafael, Florencio Lopez-De-Silanes, and Andrei Shleifer. 1999. "Corporate Ownership around the World." *Journal of Finance* 54(2):471–518.

La Porta, Rafael, Florencio Lopez-De-Silanes, Andrei Shleifer, and Robert Vishny. 1997. "Legal Determinants of External Finance." *Journal of Finance* 52(3):1131–50.

———. 1998. "Law and Finance." *Journal of Political Economy* 106(6):1113–55.

———. 2000. "Investor Protection and Corporate Governance." *Journal of Financial Economics* 58(1–2): 3–27.

———. 2002. "Investor Protection and Corporate Valuation." *Journal of Finance* 57(3):1147–70.

Lel, Ugur. 2003. "Currency Hedging, Corporate Governance and Financial Markets Development." Working Paper, Department of Finance, Indiana University, Bloomington.

Lemmon, M. L., and K. V. Lins. 2003. "Ownership Structure, Corporate Governance, and Firm Value: Evidence from the East Asian Financial Crisis." *Journal of Finance* 58(4):1445–68.

Levine, R. 1997. "Financial Development and Economic Growth: Views and Agenda." *Journal of Economic Literature* 35(2):688–726.

———. 2005. "Finance and Growth: Theory, Evidence, and Mechanisms." In P. Aghion, and S. Durlauf, eds. *Handbook of Economic Growth*. Amsterdam: North-Holland/Elsevier Publishers.

Lins, K. V. 2003. "Equity Ownership and Firm Value in Emerging Markets." *Journal of Financial and Quantitative Analysis* 38(1):159–84.

McKinsey and Company. 2002. "Global Investor Opinion Survey." [www.mckinsey.com/governance].

Mitton, T. 2002. "A Cross-Firm Analysis of the Impact of Corporate Governance on the East Asian Financial Crisis." *Journal of Financial Economics* 64(2):215–41.

Morck, Randall, Andrei Shleifer, and Robert Vishny. 1988. "Management Ownership and Market Valuation: An Empirical Analysis." *Journal of Financial Economics* 20(1):293–315.

Morck, R., B. Young, and W. Yu. 2000. "The Information Content of Stock Markets: Why Do Emerging Markets Have Synchronous Stock Price Movements?" *Journal of Financial Economics* 58(1–2):215–60.

Morck, Randall, David Stangeland, and Bernard Yeung. 2000. "Inherited Wealth, Corporate Control, and Economic Growth: The Canadian Disease." In Randall Morck, ed., *Concentrated Corporate Ownership*. National Bureau of Economic Research Conference Volume. Chicago: University of Chicago Press.

Morck, Randall, and Bernard Yeung. 2004. Family Control and the Rent-Seeking Society. *Entrepreneurship: Theory and Practice*. 28(4):391–409.

Morck, Randall, Daniel Wolfenzon, and Bernard Yeung. 2004. *Corporate Governance, Economic Entrenchment and Growth*. NBER Working Paper 10692. Cambridge, Mass.: National Bureau of Economic Research.

Nenova, T. 2003. "The Value of Corporate Votes and Control Benefits: Cross-Country Analysis." *Journal of Financial Economics* 68(3):325–51.

North, Douglass C. 1981. *Structure and Change in Economic History*. New York: Norton.

———. 1990. Institutions, Institutional Change, and Economic Performance. Cambridge: Cambridge University Press.

Pagano, Marco, and Paolo F. Volpin. 2005. "Managers, Workers, and Corporate Control." *Journal of Finance* 60(2):841–68.

Perotti, Enrico, and Ernst-Ludwig von Thadden. 2003. "The Political Economy of Bank and Equity Dominance." CEPR Discussion Paper 3914, Centre for Economic Policy Research, London.

Peters Report. 2003. *Corporate Governance in the Netherlands: Forty Recommendations*. Secretariat Committee on Corporate Governance. [www.ecgi.org].

Pistor, Katharina. 2000. "Patterns of Legal Change: Shareholder and Creditor Rights in Transition Economies." *European Business Organisation Law Review* 1(1):59–108.

Prowse, Stephen D. 1990. "Institutional Investment Patterns and Corporate Financial Behavior in the U.S. and Japan." *Journal of Financial Economics* 27(1):43–66.

Rajan, Raghuran G., and Luigi Zingales. 1998. "Which Capitalism? Lessons from the East Asian Crisis." *Journal of Applied Corporate Finance* 11(3):1–48.

———. 2003a. "The Great Reversals: The Politics of Financial Development in the 20th Century." *Journal of Financial Economics* 69(1):5–50.

———. 2003b. Saving Capitalism from the Capitalists. Unleashing the Power of Financial Markets to Create Wealth and Spread Opportunity. New York: Crown Business.

Rossi, Stefano, and Paolo Volpin. 2003. "Cross-Country Determinants of Mergers and Acquisitions." Working Paper 3889, Centre for Economic Policy Research, London.

Shleifer, Andrei, and Robert Vishny. 1997. "A Survey of Corporate Governance." *Journal of Finance* 52(2):737–83.

Siegel, Jordan. 2005. "Can Foreign Firms Bond Themselves Effectively by Submitting to U.S. Law?" *Journal of Financial Economics* 75(2):319–59.

Stulz, René, and Rohan Williamson. 2003. "Culture, Openness, and Finance." *Journal of Financial Economics* 70(3):313–49.

Tirole, Jean. 2001. "Corporate Governance." *Econometrica* 69(1):1–35.

World Bank. 2001. Finance for Growth: Policy Choices in a Volatile World. Washington, D.C.

Wurgler, Jeffrey. 2000. "Financial Markets and the Allocation of Capital." *Journal of Financial Economics* 58(1–2):1187–214.

Zingales, Luigi. 1998. "Corporate Governance." *The New Palgrave Dictionary of Economics and the Law*. London: Macmillan.

Enforcement and Good Corporate Governance in Developing Countries and Transition Economies

Erik Berglöf • Stijn Claessens

More than regulations, laws on the books, or voluntary codes, enforcement is key to creating an effective business environment and good corporate governance, at least in developing countries and transition economies. A framework is presented to help explain enforcement, the impact on corporate governance when rules are not enforced, and what can be done to improve corporate governance in weak enforcement environments. The limited empirical evidence suggests that private enforcement tools are often more effective than public tools. However, some public enforcement is necessary, and private enforcement mechanisms often require public laws to function. Private initiatives are often also taken under the threat of legislation or regulation, although in some countries bottom-up, private-led initiatives preceded and even shaped public laws. Concentrated ownership aligns incentives and encourages monitoring, but it weakens other corporate governance mechanisms and can impose significant costs. Various steps can be taken to reduce these costs and reinforce other corporate governance mechanisms. But political economy constraints, resulting from the intermingling of business and politics, often prevent improvements in the enforcement environment and the adoption and implementation of public laws.

The problem of enforcing agreements has been a long-standing part of the development agenda. Nobel laureate Douglass North (1991) argues that "how effectively agreements are enforced is the single most important determinant of economic performance." Recent research supports this assertion, suggesting that enforcement of the rule of law is perhaps the central functional difference between developed market economies and developing economies. Indeed, according to some analyses, the degree to which private property rights are respected explains the development of countries (Acemoglu, Johnson, and Robinson 2001). Comparisons between developed market economies and transition economies also show much larger differences

© The Author 2006. Published by Oxford University Press on behalf of the International Bank for Reconstruction and Development / THE WORLD BANK. All rights reserved. For permissions, please e-mail: journals.permissions@oxfordjournals.org.
doi:10.1093/wbro/lkj005   Advance Access publication 21 February 2006   21:123–150

in enforcement (law effectiveness) than in laws on the books (law extensiveness) (Pistor, Raiser, and Gelfer 2000). Simple correlations suggest that an index of the efficiency of a country's judicial systems is more strongly associated with GDP per capita than are laws protecting minority rights.

While enforcement is a general problem of development, it particularly affects firms seeking external financing. Financial contracts, after all, involve the commitment of the firm to adhere to certain obligations, in particular to pay an appropriate rate of return to the providers of external financing. A weak enforcement environment makes it more difficult for firms to make such commitments. Empirical evidence shows that actions taken against insider trading, rather than the mere presence of insider trading laws, help explain the development of securities markets (Bhattacharya and Daouk 2002). A large international study finds that the level of enforcement is more important than the quality of laws in explaining the turnover of CEOs (see Gibbons 2002; Defond and Hung 2003). This is not to say that laws are unimportant but rather to note that they need to be written so that they can be enforced and that there must be institutions to enforce them.

A weak enforcement environment also influences ownership and control patterns and the functioning of different corporate governance mechanisms. Ownership concentration and insider control are responses to the absence of other instruments by which firms can commit to lenders to repay and ensure investors of the quality of firm management. But while they can improve monitoring and align incentives, they also have many potential costs. At the firm level, these costs include entrenchment of the manager and owner; limited risk diversification; liquidity costs, as majority owners cannot easily sell their stakes; and the expropriation of minority rights. Concentrated ownership structures also undermine the effectiveness of other corporate governance mechanisms. At the country level, potential costs include undermining the development of capital markets (and the establishment of new firms), reducing access to external financing, and slowing growth. High ownership concentration also affects the development of corporate governance rules. Many, if not most, corporate governance systems in developing countries and transition economies are heavily tilted in favor of controlling owners, potentially perpetuating any social costs.

This article develops a framework to help explain enforcement, the impact on corporate governance when rules are not enforced, and what can be done to improve corporate governance in weak enforcement environments. It begins by characterizing the lack of enforcement problem and providing a typology of different forms of enforcement mechanisms. It then introduces the corporate governance problem, focusing on the role of various corporate governance mechanisms in dealing with the commitment problem of a firm seeking external financing from individual investors. After analyzing which mechanisms may be the most effective in weak contracting environments and identifying which reform options are most likely to improve corporate governance practices and mitigate social costs, the article identifies some areas for further research.

Enforcement

Although enforcement is generally agreed to be of critical importance to economic performance, and there is a vast literature on the subject, no simple framework for thinking about enforcement exists. One way of addressing the issues is to distinguish between private ordering, private enforcement of the law, public enforcement of the law, and state control (Djankov and others 2003). Private ordering initiatives are transactions that take place in the absence of laws and courts or other public enforcement institutions; they can be unilateral, bilateral, or multilateral. Private enforcement of the law occurs when private agents avail themselves of the framework defined by law or regulations to punish violations from contracts, using the courts to adjudicate and the state to enforce the final judgment. Public enforcement involves the enforcement and prosecution of the law by the government.

An aspect common to both private and public enforcement of the law is the extensiveness of the law. Law serves to standardize contracts and clarify liability, but it can be more or less extensive, affecting the nature of the enforcement problem. Government can internalize or avoid all disputes by maintaining full control and ownership over all activities.

Private Ordering

Private ordering has been the norm historically, and it remains the norm in many parts of the world today.[1] Greif (1992, 1993) provides historical examples of enforcement by traders in the Mediterranean. Ostrom, Gardner, and Walker (1990) gives illustrations from management of common resources in developing societies. Ellickson (1991) discusses the protection of property rights among cattle farmers in California. McMillan and Woodruff (1999) find evidence of private ordering in Vietnam during its transition to a market economy. Besley (1995) analyzes the protection of property rights for farmers in Ghana. Gambetta (1993) documents the role of the Sicilian mafia as a private ordering arrangement.

Unilateral enforcement mechanisms involve efforts by individual firms to improve their commitment power. Through its own actions, a firm can create valuable assets that would be lost in case of violations of earlier agreements or standards. The most common unilateral mechanism is reputation built, for example, through costly advertising.

In the absence of a well-functioning general enforcement environment, unilateral actions can be important. For example, the Russian oil company, Yukos, was generously rewarded by the stock market when it unilaterally reformed its management and corporate governance. The actions were presumably credible, because if the company, which had had a poor governance record, were to violate its professed principles, much of its investment would be lost (the investment did not, of course, protect the company and its valuation from actions by the government).

Other unilateral mechanisms include investment strategies that pay off only if the firm continues to have access to external financing. A natural resources extraction firm, for example, may undertake a large investment with a long gestation period and substantial sunk costs to signal its commitment to honoring current financial contracts, even though doing so makes it vulnerable to unanticipated future events.

If the gains from unilateral actions are so large, why do so few companies increase their commitment in this way? The greatest problem with reputation is that it relies on future interactions (such as returning to the stock market for more funding) taking place. Moreover, since the costs of building a reputation are sunk, they may not deter future violations if the gains are sufficiently large. An additional problem is that memory, particularly in stock markets, may be short. With losses to investors from previous violations already incurred and new investors coming into the market, considerations of new investments may not be affected by previous actions, thus weakening the commitment power of reputation in financial markets.

Firms can strengthen their commitment ability in their interactions through bilateral mechanisms. Reputation can play an important role in sustaining such bilateral enforcement arrangements. Yukos, for example, hired the consulting firm McKinsey to help it reform. Presumably, McKinsey would not have agreed to associate itself with the company had it not been convinced that Yukos was committed to reform.

Firms can also create vertical and horizontal dependencies in which one party gives up control over important decisions to the other party or a third party. In weak contracting environments, firms are more likely to internalize transactions, create conglomerates, or form joint ventures. Like many other companies in the Russian oil industry, Yukos integrated vertically and began building a conglomerate. It also considered many foreign joint ventures, in part to increase the costs of government intervention (the anticipation of such ventures may have contributed to the actions by the Russian government).

Joint ventures, particularly 50/50 control splits, may appear ambiguous, providing much scope for conflicts among shareholders, especially in weak contracting environments. Yet, the specific assets each partner brings in allow for commitment and optimal bilateral private contracting (see Hauswald and Hege 2003 for a formal analysis of joint ventures).

A related form of bilateral commitment is the "hostage exchange," in which one party leaves with the other assets that are more valuable to the provider than to the "hostage holder" (in medieval times princesses were used). It is difficult to find concrete examples of hostage exchanges that improve the commitment of firms toward outside third-party investors. Such exchanges are difficult to arrange, since the specific assets needed are typically in short supply and often of less value to outside investors. Some private shareholder agreements, for example, include covenants requiring some assets to be held offshore, but these are not asymmetric in value. Compensating cash balances and prepayments are sometimes cited as examples, but they are highly symmetric in value and typically require some third party, such as a bank or a court, to determine whether the party can draw on the cash balance. Moreover, timing is critical, because preferably the exchanges should be simultaneous. Bilateral mechanisms in general require some duration and reputation, and both parties should earn above-market returns to sustain the mechanism.

For external financial commitments, by far the most important class of mechanisms is multilateral arrangements. Customs among multiple parties are established over time in repeated interactions or through learning across industries and jurisdictions, as in guilds or other associations. Private parties can take the next step and establish institutions for collecting and conveying information about adherence to these customs and erect credible punishments for deviations. Intermediaries may emerge to exploit economies of scale and profit opportunities and prevent free riding in enforcement.

Examples of such mechanisms abound, although their effectiveness varies greatly. Trade associations adopt their own codes of conduct and eventually their own institutions for resolving conflicts. In the financial sector, self-regulatory organizations include brokers associations providing licenses and overseeing the conduct of brokers, investment banks establishing standards for underwriting, clearinghouses and payments systems organizing settlement and payment services, and associations of banks and other financial institutions developing rules governing conflicts of interest, exchange of information, and so forth. Intermediaries such as business organizations sell information and develop rules and standards; rating agencies and other organizations that monitor quality collect data, establish standards, and disseminate information.

Stock exchanges develop listing requirements. They develop norms for interactions among members and mechanisms for punishment. Clearinghouses, for example, expel members if necessary to function properly. Commercial and investment banks can certify and monitor firms in the context of lending and underwriting activities. Since they engage in multiple relationships, they can act as multilateral enforcement mechanisms.

Private arbitration is another form of multilateral mechanism, in which parties sign on to a mechanism that has some commitment power, as it is involved in repeated interactions. Ultimately, though, some form of public intervention enforcement may be necessary to enforce private arbitration.

Perhaps, the most important form of multilateral enforcement is self-regulation or "soft law." Key stakeholders in particular areas of economic activity come together, often with the consent or encouragement of the government, to set up and enforce rules. Self-regulatory agencies or authorities (commonly referred to as self-regulatory organizations) are created, often as complements to but sometimes as substitutes for public agencies and courts. As the jurisdiction of these agencies grows, the distinction between self-regulation and public regulation blurs. Often public regulators may surrender enforcement to self-regulatory organizations.

Private enforcement mechanisms, particularly multilateral arrangements, face many challenges. Actors should generally be expected to behave opportunistically whenever it pays. The more parties are involved, the harder it is to sustain such collaboration, unless it is supported by some form of public action. At the same time, a limited number of actors can lead to entrenchment and weaker (corporate governance and other) standards. This is particularly so in small markets, where self-regulatory associations and organizations often maintain low standards and engage in rent-seeking behavior. Reputation is also often difficult to build in developing countries and transition economies, where poor reputation makes it difficult to sustain transactions, creating fewer opportunities to build reputation. Moreover, the uncertainty that is so pervasive in these economies reduces the value of future rewards for good behavior today. When stakeholders have poor reputations and strong interests in regulatory outcomes, self-regulation may not be legitimate in the eyes of the public.

Private Enforcement of the Law

Private initiatives may require public law to be effective, and public laws and regulations may require private enforcement. The government creates the rules governing private conduct but leaves the initiation of enforcement to private parties. When a party feels cheated, it can initiate a private suit and take it to a court or other agency.

For private enforcement to be effective, agents must have incentives. Individual shareholders may not have sufficient incentives to litigate because of the free-riding problems. While procedures such as class action suits can overcome this problem, they can also lead to frivolous law suits. For many of the corporate governance issues related to securities markets, stock exchanges should have appropriate incentives to check whether firms adhere to listing standards. For many other corporate governance issues, this will not be the case.

What types of public laws lend themselves best to private enforcement of the law? In one influential view, private mechanisms are more likely to work and to be cheaper if the law mandates a certain standard. The existence of such a standard may make it easier to initiate and prove a case in court as the burden on the courts and the plaintiff of proving liability or lack of liability is reduced if statutes specify what facts need to be established. Well-defined statutes may also reduce the discretion of judges and undermine attempts to subvert the law. Some researchers have argued that private enforcement of the law may be particularly efficient in environments with weak or inexperienced courts (Black and Kraakman 1996; Hay, Shleifer, and Vishny 1996). This view, of course, assumes that private mechanisms and the setting of standards are not captured by special interests.

For private enforcement of the law to work, functioning institutions—courts, judges, and other institutions—must be able to adjudicate and impose sanctions. Governments often delegate enforcement to lower levels of government or to self-regulatory organizations. Much of the implementation of rules for, say, obtaining a business license can be delegated to semi-government agencies. Many professions, such as medicine and law, are entrusted with licensing their own members. In financial markets, many self-regulatory organizations derive their status and ability to regulate transactions from public law. A stock exchange, for example, may be granted a natural monopoly, giving it the explicit and implicit power to regulate securities markets activities.

These forms of delegated enforcement may work better if the subsidiary body has more specific information, better resources, and a broader range of sanctions. Local agencies may be better able to judge the quality of the application for a business license. Self-regulatory organizations may have better insights into what constitutes market manipulation and better information systems to detect such behavior. Self-regulatory organizations may also be able to delicense, issue reprimands ("name and shame"), and impose financial sanctions, actions that may be more difficult for a government agency.

In most cases, failure to comply with sanctions imposed by the delegated enforcers triggers actions by the public sector. These agencies therefore need some backing up from higher levels of government or the judicial system.

Public Enforcement of the Law

A large body of literature examines public enforcement of the law (see, Polinsky and Shavell 2000, for a review). This section focuses on three of the issues it addresses: the interrelationship between the extensiveness and the effectiveness of law, the positive theory of enforcement and the efficiency and effectiveness of enforcement institutions, and the relationships between laws, corruption, and enforcement.

Many laws are unwritten, so the first question that arises is what needs to be codified, how codification varies across countries, and how codification interacts with the various enforcement mechanisms. Very homogenous and close-knit societies may still be able to rely on social means to enforce norms of behavior. As they develop more market-based economies, with arm's length contracts, they require more formality and codification in the forms of laws.

In the simplest possible characterization, written laws (and regulations) have no independent function; the only thing that matters is that part of the laws and regulations that is actually enforced. Some argue that this dichotomy is too simple: the written law can be more or less extensive, enforcement can be more or less effective, and the extensiveness of the law can affect the nature of the enforcement problem. Under this view, one can think of a two-by-two matrix with rudimentary versus extensive rules and weak versus strong enforcement, with costs and benefits in each of the four cells. A large literature has documented differences between the extensiveness of the law (that is, the scope and detail of the law) and its effectiveness (that is, the extent to which the law is actually enforced). Since each law and regulation has its own optimal balance, the distinction between written rules and their enforcement becomes blurred.

A related view distinguishes between low and high legal standards, where the distinction relates to the threshold set for violating the law. This body of work examines the choice between very detailed, highly nuanced rules and simple, easily understood and interpreted rules (so-called "bright-line" rules). Some laws are more easily enforced than others, suggesting that the enforcement environment may shape what laws are desirable and that how the law is written may in turn influence the scope for enforcement. With imprecise laws, for example, private ordering and private enforcement may be costly or uncertain, and the benefits for parties to deviate may be too great.

For this reason, Glaeser and Shleifer (2001) argue in favor of bright-line rules in securities markets. At the same time, broader laws allow for more evolution. The tradeoff between the strictness of the laws and the incentives to comply has been used in the debate on accounting principles, where the choice has been between international accounting standards, which are more principle based, and the U.S. Financial Accounting Standards Board norms, which are more detailed and rule based.

The tradeoff has also been at the center of the general economic literature on (public) enforcement, inspired by Gary Becker's (1968) provocative article suggesting that maximizing punishment would ensure optimal enforcement. Later contributions have emphasized the constraints imposed on fines by the wealth of those punished. Others have pointed to the (exogenous) limits to enforcement technology. These analyses have provided some insights into the factors affecting enforcement technology and the choice among enforcement technologies.

The efficiency and effectiveness of technologies and enforcement institutions such as courts (but also regulators, stock exchanges, self-regulatory organizations, and the like) are hard to study empirically. Efficiency normally refers to outputs relative to inputs, but both outputs and inputs are difficult to measure. In evaluating the efficiency of courts, the speed with which cases are processed cannot be the only criterion. Access (by the poor, for example); fairness; and predictability are also important. In some cases, effectiveness may also be the overriding objective, and very large sums may be justified to ensure that an outcome is just or right. The Microsoft antitrust cases in the United States and European Union, for example, cost taxpayers millions of dollars, but the expenditures may have been worthwhile given the enormous implications of the case.

How cases are managed—that is, what input (judicial systems, legal assistance) is entered when—also matters. Input efficiency involves assessing the type of funding and incentives provided. Ultimately, court output must take into account overall customer satisfaction, that is, the degree to which people trust the legal system. Analysis of court efficiency needs to extend beyond the courts to understand their role in the larger legal system. Much more conceptual and empirical work is needed on how to evaluate courts.

A body of literature exists on the importance for enforcement of regulators and supervisors that are independent, have adequate powers, are well staffed, and have operational and financial functional independence. Evidence of its importance has been found for central banks and other agencies, such as competition policy agencies and regulatory agencies. Financial and operational independence can be particularly important but dependent on subtle rules. In many countries, securities exchange regulators have their own sources of income (fees from new issues or trading), but they have to transfer some part to the general budget or have their budget approved by the parliament or other government agencies, thus reducing their de facto independence.

At the same time, there can be limits to the benefits of stronger regulators and supervisors in the weak institutional environments of many developing countries. Greater legal powers in environments with relatively low pay for regulators and supervisors and weak checks and balances may create perverse effects, as Barth, Caprio, and Levine (2004) note. In such environments, giving more powers to public enforcers may simply invite more corruption.

The Choice of Enforcement Technologies

All enforcement mechanisms have costs and benefits, and both complementary and tradeoff relationships exist. Private and public initiatives are often complements rather than substitutes. For example, the effectiveness of private enforcement mechanisms often depends on the effectiveness of public enforcement mechanisms. Public enforcement can also reduce the costs of private enforcement. But while more public intervention may mitigate market failure, it is more vulnerable to government failure, and it may not be most efficient when private agents have better information, resources, and incentives. Tradeoffs can arise. Private agents are particularly important for enforcement when the general institutional environment is weak. A system of social control of business is necessary where both markets and government fail or cannot be expected to operate.

The preferred mix of enforcement technologies varies by type of activity and country characteristics. In some areas, social norms serve as the first enforcement technology, with the more formal system used as a second resort. The media can play an important role, both nationally and locally. Consumer actions can also be important, even for corporate governance. Threats of revolts by customers against a large pay package for the new CEO of the Dutch grocery chain Albert Heijn led the company to reduce his pay package and the chairman of the board of directors of the parent group (Ahold) to resign. In many ways, these social pressures are the most important corporate governance mechanisms. They require relatively free media and access to newspapers. Technology can also be important, as it has been in the Republic of Korea, where concerns about corporations' activities have been shared over the Internet.

Although it is hard to generalize, the role various formal enforcement technologies play in a particular sector or activity depends in part on the relative costs and benefits of these technologies. The existence of cheaper outside options affects the use of courts versus other enforcement technologies, such as arbitrage in commercial disputes. The choice of mechanism also depends on the extent to which one technology requires the backing of another to make it credible and ensure finality of decision. Activist movements, such as shareholder lobbying groups, require some legal backing (Milhaupt 2003). Regulatory intervention in the corporate governance area does not typically fully resolve the basic commitment problem and requires some backing by the court system for appeals and enforcement (insider trading pursued by the stock exchange requires the backing of sanctions by a securities and exchange commission, for example). An important corporate governance mechanism is monitoring by banks, but the development of bank lending and monitoring obviously relies on the effectiveness of the regulatory framework and supervision, in addition to other public enforcement institutions that allow collateral to be collected.

How effective are private mechanisms—unilateral, bilateral, or multilateral—in bringing about change in enforcement of good governance practices? Black (2001) provides some suggestive data from the Russian Federation indicating that even in a weak environment, individual firms can increase their value substantially by improving their corporate governance unilaterally. Firms in Central and Eastern Europe sometimes voluntarily disclose more information than is required (Berglöf and Pajuste 2005). Similar evidence exists for the Korea (Black, Jang, and Kim 2003) and other countries. Serious causality and other methodological problems weaken the power of these studies, however.

The entry of foreign firms, which normally adhere to higher governance standards, can also help. Cross-border mergers and acquisitions tend to originate in countries with higher corporate governance standards, potentially improving corporate governance in the partner countries (Rossi and Volpin 2003). There is also a tendency, however, for foreign investors to adjust to or even misuse the local corporate governance environment, as the takeover of firms in developing countries and transition economies by foreign investors at "unfair" values has shown. Even if incentives are weak for individual firms, foreign (and domestic) entry and competition may nevertheless put pressure on local firms to improve their corporate governance.

The effectiveness of all of these private enforcement mechanisms in the area of corporate governance depends on the institutional environment. Private mechanisms are complements to public enforcement. Private arbitration, for example, is more likely to be effective when courts and enforcement agencies work well. In work on Korea Black, Jang, and Kim (2003) show that private mechanisms are often insufficient and need the support of government intervention. Durnev and Kim (2005) and Klapper and Love (2003) suggest that actions by individual firms cannot compensate fully for deficiencies in local governance practices.

Private enforcement mechanisms are nevertheless likely to be the main mechanisms in most markets, particularly in countries with severe weaknesses in public law and public enforcement. Evidence is still limited, but in the area of securities regulation, private enforcement of the law seems highly effective for capital market development, while public enforcement seems less important (La Porta, Lopez-de-Silanes, and Shleifer 2006). As many elements of securities regulation involve issues related to corporate governance, this may apply to enforcement of corporate governance more generally (Lopez-de-Silanes 2004). Furthermore, in one view, public law emerges out of private ordering, at least in common law systems; courts "find" well-functioning contractual arrangements and elevate them to law (Cooter 1991). The history of securities law in the United States seems to confirm this view, in that private parties adopted rules that later were adopted by individual market places and eventually became laws or regulations. Coffee (1999, 2002) reviews the effects of globalization of securities markets on corporate governance standards and the spread (or lack thereof) of international standards.

To some extent, cost-benefit considerations can explain the choices among enforcement technologies. Path dependence is also important, however, an enforcement technology may be introduced and then remain in use for a long time, even though other, more efficient paperless technologies have become available. For example, collateral (the registration of the title of the asset to ensure that rights are unequivocal) is a form of contract enforcement. Today, collateral can be registered electronically and perfected using registries rather than expensive courts or notary-based systems, but the transition to electronic systems often takes time, and institutional reluctance may have to be overcome. Technological progress can change enforcement tools. Securitization, the sale of many assets bundled together, became possible only as a result of progress in information technology that allowed secondary asset sales while ensuring that the underlying contracts remained identifiable and could be enforced.

The mix of technologies in many developing countries and transition economies differs from that observed in developed countries. Public enforcement can play only a limited role in weak institutional environments, as powerful insiders will most likely find their way around the system. Private enforcement of public laws and the power of litigation and court intervention vary greatly across countries as well, in large part depending on the functioning of the public enforcement institutions. Russian investors, for example, almost never go to court, because the likelihood of success there is miniscule and even if they win, the judgment is often not enforced (Zhuravskaya and Zamulin 2003). Yet, even here relative costs are important. In China, more and more investors are taking their grievances to court, even though court decisions are not always predictable or necessarily enforced (Pistor and Xu 2003). The reason is that other mechanisms are absent or even more costly. Weaknesses in public enforcement are also likely to foster the growth of other mechanisms including informal, mafia-type mechanisms.

Many of the choices between technologies depend less on the specific activity and more on the overall economic environment. Several interrelated factors then come into play. Slinko, Yakovlev, and Zhuravskaya (2002) show that the general environment of courts and other enforcement institutions is affected by the incentives of national and local authorities, political competition at various levels of government, and the strength of civil society. These aspects vary not only across countries but also across regions and municipalities within a country. Large differences exist in enforcement among states or provinces not only in the Russian Federation but also in countries like Brazil and Mexico (Broadman 1999; Pinheiro Castelar and Cabral 2001; Laeven and Woodruff 2003). Furthermore, where markets function poorly, it is more difficult for the legal system to function, as the standard against which to judge financial and economic aspects of transactions is unclear. Conversely, increases in competition in product markets, which affect the scope for capture, and the size of the small and medium-size enterprise sector, which affects the role of insiders, can affect the functioning of courts. Policies promoting bank lending and financial development may also help.

Initial conditions, endowments, and the distribution of natural resources and technology also matter for the institutional development of countries including the degree of public enforcement. The historical origin of the legal and general institutional system (English, French, German, or Scandinavian) and the corresponding basic legal mechanism (common law or civil law) seem to matter for enforcement (Glaeser and Shleifer 2002). Relationships have been found between institutional features and countries' more permanent characteristics, including culture, history, and physical endowments. Institutional characteristics, such as the risk of expropriation of private property, can be long lasting and relate to a country's physical endowments (Acemoglu, Johnson, and Robinson 2001). Both a country's initial endowments and the origin of its legal systems are important determinants of the degree of private property rights protection (Beck, Demirgüç-Kunt, and Levine 2003). Wholesale legal transplants are largely ineffective in diffusing enforcement practices (Berkowitz, Pistor, and Richard 2003).

The general enforcement environment is the product not only of many different market, endowment, and legal factors but also of social and cultural factors. Enforcement depends on basic social norms and trust (Djankov and others 2003, refer to this as "civic capital"). When societies are socially and culturally heterogeneous, the base for natural forms of enforcement is typically weaker. This is clearly true at the micro level: the ability to operate well-functioning rotating saving schemes, for example, greatly depends on the presence of close relationships and homogenous groups (see Berglöf, Burkart, and Friebel 2003). But it also seems true at the country level, where the roles of culture and openness have been found to be important for financial sector development including for corporate governance (Stulz and Williamson 2003). As societies develop, though, and undergo both economic and social transformation, the nature and forms of enforcement are likely to change toward more formal modes.

Political institutions are part of the general enforcement environment. They may not function well, and they can be dominated by an absolute ruler or captured by special interests. In both cases, serious enforcement problems can result. Countries with absolute rulers face many public governance issues including the protection of property rights against interference by the dictator. These countries may have fewer enforcement issues, however, as there are few genuine "market" transactions (Acemoglu and Johnson 2003). The other set of countries includes those, such as many emerging markets, in which business and politics tend to merge. When the rich influence the path of justice, litigation does not work (Glaeser, Sheinkman, and Shleifer 2003). When enforcement institutions are corrupt, the level of enforcement may be endogenous (Acemoglu and Verdier 2000). Corruption lowers the effectiveness of enforcement by increasing the costs of motivating and monitoring bureaucrats. When large controlling owners become politicians, an important countervailing force to government is lost and the interests of minority shareholders are less likely to be protected.

Legal standards and the level of enforcement can interact. Governments may respond to weak enforcement by establishing codes to reduce discretion and opportunities for subverting the law, but this can have its own costs. Stricter laws and regulations offer more incentives to evade and thus are more costly to enforce. Corruption may affect how laws are written (Immordino and Pagano 2003).[2] In this view, legal standards and enforcement are complements; as countries develop, both can increase.

Laws and regulations can be adopted not only to correct market failures, reduce transactions costs, and achieve social objectives but also to extract bribes. Djankov and others (2002) find some support for this "tollbooth view," especially in developing countries, suggesting that policymakers should err on the side of less strict or extensive laws in weaker environments. Barth, Caprio, and Levine (2004) find that giving more powers to bank supervisors leads to less efficient and more unstable financial systems in environments with limited checks and balances. Immordino and Pagano (2003) provide evidence that governments in developing countries adopt lower standards to avoid the higher enforcement costs of stricter standards.

Enforcement and Corporate Governance

Private ordering, private law enforcement, and public law enforcement all play a role in determining the overall effectiveness of the business environment. The different sets of mechanisms overlap and can both substitute for and reinforce one another. To evaluate how the various options interact, the main corporate governance problem in developing countries and transition economies needs to be defined.[3] This section focuses on how a weak general enforcement environment influences the basic corporate governance mechanisms. (For reviews of the corporate governance literature, see Shleifer and Vishny 1997 and Becht, Bolton, and Roell 2003; for a review that focuses on developing countries and transition economies, see the article by Claessens in this volume.)

An entrepreneur or manager approaching outside markets for finance faces a serious commitment problem: how can investors be assured that he will choose the right projects, exert sufficient effort, adequately disclose relevant information, and ultimately repay investors? In the complete absence of credible commitment, outside investors assume the worst case scenario, that is, that the entrepreneur/manager will use all opportunities to defraud investors or in other ways not live up to his promises. The weaker the entrepreneur/manager's commitment power, the costlier outside financing (and the more difficult it will be to recruit good personnel and establish long-term relationships with suppliers and customers). Corporate governance is in great part about mitigating this commitment problem. In fact, this is the definition of *corporate governance* Shleifer and Vishny advance in their 1997 review: "Corporate governance deals with the ways in which suppliers of finance to corporations assure themselves of getting a return on their investment" (1997, p. 737).

Investors can reduce the likelihood of being defrauded or deceived by monitoring and potentially punishing management. Firms can try to employ a variety of commitment mechanisms to overcome investors' concerns. But problems arise for two reasons. The first is that an individual investor may not face the proper incentives to pay the costs involved in ensuring that the entrepreneur/manager lives up to his promises and may attempt to free ride on monitoring and enforcement by other investors. The second is that the mechanisms to commit and punish may be missing or incomplete, possibly due to poor enforcement of property rights in the country. Typically, the two problems go together.

The most common response to the free rider and poor contracting problems is to give one shareholder a sufficiently large stake in the firm so as to provide him with incentives to monitor and intervene when necessary. Concentration is often further reinforced as control is increased beyond direct ownership, primarily through pyramiding but in some countries also through cross-ownership and dual class shares. In fact, the overwhelming majority of companies in developing countries and transition economies have highly concentrated control (La Porta, Lopez-de-Silanes, and Shleifer 1999).[4] Some controlling shareholdings have their origins in (individual or family-owned) firms that grew and accessed public markets while leaving the original owners with close control. But investors also respond to weak contracting environments by building up controlling stakes that are sufficiently large as to provide proper incentives to monitor management. In Central and Eastern Europe, for example, where shareholdings were initially deliberately widely dispersed, shareholdings have consolidated to concentration levels exceeding those in Western Europe and comparable to those in many developing countries (Berglöf and Pajuste 2003).

Concentrated control is a solution to some corporate governance problems. It reduces the precommitment problem in one dimension, by reducing the demand for external financing. Combined with control and a direct role in management, it also overcomes some of the principal agent and ex post resolution problems. Management, for example, becomes easier to oversee with a single controlling shareholder, and oversight is not a problem if management and the controlling owners are identical. At the same time, there are important costs associated with ownership concentration (Morck and Yeung 2003). Such delegation of authority gives rise to the problem of monitoring the large shareholder. The large shareholder may be entrenched and optimize private benefits rather than shareholder value, and he may expropriate minority shareholders by channeling the firm's resources to his own account and using other mechanisms.

In weak contracting environments, controlling shareholders are most often the inevitable outcome. Unlike some developed countries, notably the United Kingdom and the United States, where the overriding corporate governance conflicts are between powerful managers and widely dispersed investors, the main corporate governance conflict in most countries pits controlling shareholders against minority shareholders. Corporate governance policy has to strike a balance between providing benefits to the controlling shareholders and protecting minority investors. To the extent that ownership and management have been separated, there are also potential conflicts between controlling shareholders and management and between minority shareholders and management. While many if not most corporate governance systems in developing countries and transition economies are heavily tilted in favor of controlling owners, wholesale transfer of governance standards from developed market economies may discourage investors from taking controlling positions and thus possibly undermine the most potent corporate governance mechanism in developing economies.

The presence of large blockholders, while inevitable in weak contracting environments, undermines some corporate governance mechanisms (for a review of various corporate governance mechanisms, see Becht, Bolton, and Roell 2003). Both takeover bids and proxy fights with the controlling shareholder are less likely to succeed when shareholdings are concentrated. The market for corporate control never materializes as insiders cannot be challenged. Similarly, board activism is less likely to be successful in challenging the dominant owner, given that the owner appoints the board. Executive compensation schemes are also less important as governance mechanisms when controlling investors can easily intervene more directly and oust management or controlling owners are themselves managers.

The relative importance of a particular corporate governance mechanism also depends on the enforcement environment in a country. Many firms in developed countries are closely held, but minority investors have some means to challenge insiders and ensure a reasonable rate of return on their investment. As a result, they are willing to provide external financing. In environments in which the court system functions satisfactorily, formal protection of minority shareholders enforced through private litigation is an option for improving the functioning of the key mechanisms of large shareholder monitoring. In weaker enforcement environments, policy may have to focus on promoting private mechanisms and empowering shareholders by disseminating information. The priorities for corporate governance reform and the scope for impact of policy intervention must thus take into account the environment, as the effectiveness of these other mechanisms hinges on the general and specific enforcement environment.

The effectiveness of various corporate governance mechanisms varies, and each has different scope for policy intervention (table 1). Different forms of private and public enforcement reinforce different corporate governance mechanisms. Some of these mechanisms are discussed below.

Large Shareholders

When the general enforcement environment is weak, external finance is costly, resulting in ownership concentration. Controlling shareholders are thus a feature of weak environments, a fact that any attempt to improve corporate governance has to take into account. Large shareholders act in their own interests and may pursue private benefits rather than increase overall firm value or the rates of return to minority shareholders. State ownership or covenants giving the state-specific (veto) rights (so-called golden shares) can, in some circumstances, be a means of dealing with the social costs of weak enforcement settings.

Table 1. Corporate Governance Mechanisms and Enforcement

Corporate governance mechanism	Private ordering	Enforcement mechanism		Importance in developing countries and transition economies	Possible policy interventions
		Private law enforcement	Public law enforcement		
Blockholders	Natural consequence of weak enforcement	(Minority) shareholder suits	Governance codes evolving into corporate and securities law	Likely to be most important governance mechanism	Strengthen rules protecting minority investors without removing incentives to hold controlling blocks
Market for corporate control			Corporate law (defenses, procedural rules); transparency of ownership and control	Unlikely to be important when ownership is strongly concentrated; can still take place through debt contracts but requires bankruptcy system	Remove some managerial defenses, require disclosure of ownership and control, develop banking system
Proxy fights			Improved communication technology; voting by mail	Unlikely to be effective when ownership is strongly concentrated	Improve technology for communicating with and among shareholders, require disclosure of ownership and control
Board activity	Interaction among board members, training of independent directors			Unlikely to be influential when controlling owner can hire and fire board members	Introduce elements of independence of directors, training of directors, require disclosure of voting, allow cumulative voting
Executive compensation	Transparency rules of stock exchanges		Transparency rules	Less important when controlling owner can hire and fire and has private benefits	Require disclosure of compensation schemes, conflicts of interest rules

(Continued)

Table 1. (Continued)

Corporate governance mechanism	Enforcement mechanism				Possible policy interventions
	Private ordering	Private law enforcement	Public law enforcement	Importance in developing countries and transition economies	
Monitoring by banks	Credit bureaus, registries, reputation		Protection of collateral; bankruptcy reform	Important but depends on health of banking system and regulatory environment	Strengthen banking regulation and institutions, encourage accumulation of information on credit histories, develop supporting credit bureaus and other information intermediaries
Shareholder activism	No ownership limits		Requirement to disclose voting and positions of institutional investors	Potentially important, particularly in large firms with dispersed shareholders	Encourage interaction among shareholders, strengthen minority protection, enhance governance of institutional investors
Monitoring by employees	Labor flexibility			Potentially very important, particularly in smaller companies with high-skilled human capital, where threat of leaving is high	Require disclosure of information to employees, consider requiring board representation, ensure flexible labor markets
Litigation		Key mechanism for private enforcement	Governance codes adopted by exchanges and others that have a "charter" provided by law	Depends critically on quality of general enforcement environment but can sometimes work	Facilitate communication among shareholders, encourage class action suits, with safeguards against excessive litigation

Table 1. (Continued)

Corporate governance mechanism	Enforcement mechanism			Importance in developing countries and transition economies	Possible policy interventions
	Private ordering	Private law enforcement	Public law enforcement		
Reputation and self-enforcement	Depending on growth opportunities and degree of rents			Important when general enforcement is weak, stronger when environment is stronger	Encourage competition in factor markets
Media and social control	Deregulation of media to allow freer competition			Potentially important but depends on competition among and independence of media	Encourage competition in and diverse control of media (active public campaigns can empower public)
Bilateral private enforcement mechanisms	Hostage and shareholders agreements. Require firm-specific assets.	Establishment of specific control rights under contract law		Important, as they can be more specific generic corporate governance rules, but mechanisms do not benefit outsiders and can have downsides.	Develop functioning civil/commercial courts.
Arbitration, auditing, and other multilateral mechanisms	Arbitration to resolve conflicts; other third parties (auditors, rating agencies); stock exchange listing requirements; foreign listings; trade organizations; and corporate governance codes for reputation, signaling, standardization of norms			Potentially important—often the origin of public law—but enforcement problem often remains; audits sometimes abused; conflicts of interest a potential problem	Facilitate formation of private third-party mechanisms (to mitigate the need to form public alternatives where possible), deal with conflicts of interest, ensure competition

Market for Corporate Control

The market for corporate control is less active, making hostile takeovers less effective and proxy fights more difficult to win. Hostile takeovers are not completely impossible, however. In the Russian Federation, for example, investors have found ways to exploit financial distress and use bankruptcy rules to topple incumbent owner-managers (Guriev and others 2003). Whether this is leading to efficient outcomes remains to be seen, but it shows that some elements of a market for control are working.

Board Activity

Since owners appoint boards, little independent corporate governance should be expected from the board in a firm with a controlling owner. Requiring independent directors has limited direct effect as the controlling shareholder will not allow any real influence on the firm's board. Nevertheless, requiring some degree of independence from some directors could still be important. For example, independent directors can play an important role in transferring knowledge at the level of the individual firm and building constituencies for corporate governance reform at the country level.

Executive Compensation

Executive compensation schemes do not play the same role in decisionmaking as they do in firms with more dispersed ownership structures, given that the controlling owner can hire and fire managers at his discretion. Furthermore, the controlling shareholder typically has many other means to "reward" himself. Disclosure of executive compensation schemes is nevertheless a good thing, even when it is not the key motivating force in managerial decisionmaking, as public pressure may help restrain some forms of dilution. More generally, transparency promotes an informed discussion of corporate governance at both the firm and the country level.

Monitoring by Banks

Lending by banks is typically the most important source of external finance. As lenders, banks have a direct stake in the governance of corporations, requiring firm behavior that ensures that their loans will be repaid. As monitors, banks can compensate for some weaknesses in the general enforcement environment, as they have repeated dealings, have a reputation to maintain in lending, and can economize on monitoring and enforcement technology. The development of bank lending itself obviously relies on the effectiveness of the regulatory framework and supervision, in addition to other institutions that allow collateral to be collected. Public enforcement is therefore still a necessity.

Shareholder groups, which exist in Japan, Korea, the United Kingdom, the United States, and many other countries, can also be important. The effectiveness of such groups varies, depending on their funding structures, whether awards are distributed to members or kept for future activities, and whether they seek to use and improve existing local enforcement institutions or abandon them, as Milhaupt (2003) shows in an analysis of shareholder groups organized as nonprofit organizations in Japan, Korea, and Taiwan (China).

Monitoring by Employees

Monitoring by employees can be an effective mechanism for enhancing corporate governance, as the interests of employees are largely aligned with good firm performance and fair treatment of all stakeholders. For this mechanism to be powerful, employees must be mobile, however, so that their threat to leave the firm is credible. More generally, effective competition in all factor markets improves firm's corporate governance. Increased competition in output markets not only puts more pressure on the firm to enhance its performance, it also increases the premium on better corporate governance to be able to attract the necessary financing to invest and survive.

Litigation

Litigation cannot be expected to be a good governance mechanism in weak contracting environments. It is, however, less dependent on government actions than public enforcement, as it is a form of private enforcement of public laws. In securities markets, private enforcement works better than public enforcement, especially in developing countries (La Porta, Lopez-de-Silanes, and Shleifer 2005). Litigation can also help develop the standards against which corporations know they will be judged and which may eventually evolve into law.

Media and Social Control

Media and social control often play an important role in disciplining managers and controlling owners (Dyck and Zingales 2003). Such control improves access to information, reduces the costs of monitoring, and makes corporate governance an issue of public debate. In countries such as Korea, corporate governance became a household word thanks in part to wide media coverage of corporate sector abuses. In turn, regulation and other efforts promoting plurality in media can have a strong impact on the enforcement of good corporate governance.

Reputation

Even when ownership and control in individual firms are concentrated, because of weak enforcement, reputation mechanisms can be of value for large shareholders, because the firms need to raise outside funds. But minority shareholders should not expect too much from formal governance mechanisms.

Bilateral Private Enforcement Mechanism

Most private agreements are bilateral. To be renegotiated ex post when they are not enforced, they require firm-specific assets. Moreover, they need not benefit other shareholders. Nevertheless, bilateral agreements may be valuable (to blockholders) even in the absence of firm-specific assets. While they suffer from the weaknesses in the general contracting environment, agreements between blockholders and the controlling shareholder, which may cover board representation, access to information, permission for changes in control rights, and procedures for approving related party transactions, can add value. Because they include more specific covenants, they may overcome some incompleteness in the existing legal system and can more easily be judged by inexperienced courts. In addition, the general court system dealing with civil cases may be better than the specific court system dealing with capital market transactions. In many developing countries and transition economies, for example, civil courts function relatively well, but courts that deal with capital market transactions do not. In case of such "arbitrage" opportunities, shareholders' agreements can add value to blockholders. They are of little value, however, to small shareholders.

Arbitration, Auditing, and Other Multilateral Mechanisms

For joint ventures or international investments, arbitration can help enforcement, as it can rely on tools such as the New York Convention, which makes international arbitration binding in the local context (although it still requires some degree of local enforcement). Arbitration is of less value, however, when the general enforcement environment is weak and backup and appeal procedures are missing. Only in markets with repeated dealings and a small number of participants can arbitration work well.

The listing requirements of stock exchanges are another multilateral tool. Brazil's Novo Mercado combines higher corporate governance standards with an arbitrage system. Provision of voluntary standards can be useful, although they require some enforcement. Their effectiveness depends on the "franchise value" of the exchange: if the exchange is a (local) monopoly, it may have more enforcement power. (At the same time, the stock exchange may be less interested in corporate governance reform.) On other stock exchanges, listing rules are forcing corporations to reform or risk delisting and seeing their access to public market financing disappear. Still, the effort needs to improve over other options for firms to signal higher corporate governance standards such as using international markets. Listing on a foreign stock exchange can be a bonding device as it involves some costs to adhere to higher standards. Some researchers note, however, that the securities and exchange commissions of host countries often do not take actions against minority rights violations committed at home (see Siegel 2005 for the case of Mexico; Licht 2003). As with the general findings for securities markets, listing abroad may help more through private enforcement of exchange listing requirements, particularly disclosure, and for only some aspects of public laws.

Other third parties can help by bonding. Accountants and auditors can signal the quality of a corporation and some of its corporate governance aspects if they have some reputation to lose. The scope for accounting and auditors to improve governance depends partly on the local standards used in accounting and auditing and the legal liabilities for misrepresentation. Accounting and auditing firms can suffer from conflicts of interest if they have other business, such as consulting contracts, with the same firm. Investment banks can signal the quality of firms in the process of underwriting public offerings, although here, too, conflicts of interest can lower the value of the signal.

Rating agencies assess firms for bond and loan ratings, which include some assessment of their corporate governance. Recently, traditional rating agencies and others have produced corporate governance ratings of firms. These ratings can coordinate information collection, establish standards, and be a source of bonding when rating agencies have reputations to protect. These ratings are new and have yet to prove their value, but they could be particularly useful for institutional investors that cannot incur the costs of assessing the corporate governance of each individual firm.

Like corporate governance ratings, corporate governance codes can coordinate information collection and establish standards. Stock exchanges can use them as part of their listing requirements ("comply or explain"), giving codes some enforcement power. Codes can also have an indirect value if they lead to the codification of laws. They do not enforce laws by themselves, however, and need to be used by investors and others to induce changes in the behavior of corporations.

Conclusions

Given the lack of research on enforcement and corporate governance, it is very difficult to draw strong conclusions. Some general lessons can be drawn, however, not all of them limited to enforcement.

One observation is that private sector efforts to enhance enforcement are often more effective than government-led efforts, but the two forms of enforcement tend to complement each other. Private ordering can precede and serve as a basis for public laws and a model for private and public enforcement of these laws. The balance between private ordering and private enforcement of public laws depends on the quality of public laws and the strength of enforcement institutions. When the general enforcement environment is very weak, private ordering may be the only hope. With a better contracting environment, the evidence, at least from securities regulation, suggests that private enforcement can be important.

Improvements in enforcement are more often the result of bottom-up approaches than top-down efforts. Capacity building is often important to support private initiatives (from rating agencies to banks), and it can help build constituencies for reform. Top-down efforts to improve the legal and enforcement environment are difficult and rarely successful. The record of transplanting elements of foreign legal systems has not been a good one, but the experience of EU accession suggests that outside anchors can play a positive role in enhancing reforms.

Enforcement greatly matters for corporate governance and for the ability of the corporate sector to attract external financing and improve its performance and growth. When designing strategies for improving enforcement of corporate governance, policymakers should consider both the likely impact of a governance mechanism and the scope for improving the mechanism. A particular mechanism may play a very important role in reducing agency costs, but it may have little room for improving enforcement or vice versa.

Knowledge about enforcement is limited; most issues need to be researched further. In particular, better understanding is needed of the balance between private and public enforcement of public standards. The empirical work on securities market laws shows the benefits of relying more on private means in enforcing some minority shareholder rights, disclosure, and other regulations to develop capital markets. But the conceptual basis for this observation remains weak. Investigation of the issue for other aspects of corporate governance is needed.

It would also be useful to better understand the effectiveness of self-regulatory agencies and organizations in encouraging better standards and stricter enforcement of these standards. When, for example, are stock exchanges effective in promoting good corporate governance? What does the move to a more for-profit status mean for the incentive structures of stock exchanges to adopt higher corporate governance standards? What other self-regulatory organizations can be effective and under what conditions?

Notes

Erik Berglöf is chief economist of the European Bank for Reconstruction and Development, a professor, and director of the Stockholm Institute for Transition Economies at the Stockholm School of Economics and a fellow of the Centre for Economic Policy Research; his e-mail address is erik.berglof@hhs.se. Stijn Claessens is a professor of international finance policy at the University of Amsterdam, senior adviser to the Financial Sector Vice-Presidency of the World Bank, and a fellow of the Centre for Economic Policy Research; his e-mail address is sclaessens@worldbank.org. This article was prepared for the Global Corporate Governance Forum. The authors owe Katharina Pistor many thanks for her extensive comments. They also thank the participants in the World Bank workshop on "Enforcement in Corporate Governance," held in Washington, D.C., June 19, 2003; the participants in the workshop on enforcement held during the Global Corporate Governance Forum High-Level Working Meeting and Consultation on the OECD Corporate Governance Principles, held in Paris, November 2–4, 2003; and various seminar participants and three referees for very useful comments and suggestions.

1. For a general review of private ordering, see Dixit (2004).

2. In the model of Immordino and Pagano, a benevolent government trades off the benefits of stricter legal standards for the costs of their enforcement. With a benevolent government, standards should be set lower, because the costs of enforcing them are higher.

3. For simplicity, developing countries and transition economies are not distinguished here, even though the problems they face often differ in nature (for a discussion of the different corporate challenges facing developing countries and transition economies, see Berglöf and von Thadden 2000). Recently, there has been some convergence between the two types of economies, in terms of ownership concentration, for example (Berglöf and Pajuste 2003).

4. Many firms in developed countries are also closely controlled (Becht and Mayer, 2001; Faccio and Lang 2002).

References

Acemoglu, Daron, and Thierry Verdier. 2000. "The Choice Between Market Failures and Corruption." *American Economic Review Papers and Proceedings* 90(1):194–211.

Acemoglu, Daron, and Simon Johnson. 2003. "Unbundling Institutions." NBER Working Paper 9934. Cambridge, Mass.: National Bureau of Economic Research.

Acemoglu, Daron, Simon Johnson, and James A. Robinson. 2001. "The Colonial Origins of Comparative Development: An Empirical Investigation." *American Economic Review* 91(5):1369–1401.

Barth, James R., Gerard Caprio Jr., and Ross Levine. 2004. "Bank Regulation and Supervision: What Works Best?" *Journal of Financial Intermediation* 13(2):205–48.

Becht, Marco, and Colin Mayer. 2001. "The Control of Corporate Europe." In Fabrizio Barca and Marco Becht, eds, *The Control of Corporate Europe*. Oxford: Oxford University Press.

Becht, Marco, Patrick Bolton, and Ailsa Roell. 2003. "Corporate Governance and Control." In George Constantinides, Milton Harris, and René Stulz, eds, *Handbook of the Economics of Finance*. Amsterdam: North-Holland.

Beck, Thorsten, Asli Demirgüç-Kunt, and Ross Levine. 2003. "Law, Endowments, and Finance." *Journal of Financial Economics* 70(2):137–81.

Becker, Gary. 1968. "Crime and Punishment: An Economic Approach." *Journal of Political Economy* 76(2):169–217.

Berglöf, E., and Ernst-Ludwig von Thadden. 2000. "The Changing Corporate Governance Paradigm." In B. Pleskovic and J. Stiglitz, eds, *World Development Conference*. Washington, D.C.: World Bank.

Berglöf, E., and A. Pajuste. 2003. "Corporate Governance in Central and Eastern Europe." In P. Cornelius and B. Kogut, eds, *Global Competitiveness and Corporate Governance*. Oxford: Oxford University Press.

———. 2005. "What do Firms Disclose and Why? Enforcing Corporate Governance and Transparency in Central and Eastern Europe." Working Paper. Stockholm: Stockholm School of Economics and Stockholm Institute of Transition Economics.

Berglöf, E., M. Burkart, and G. Friebel. 2003. "Clubs-in-Clubs: Enforcement Under Unanimity." Working Paper. Stockholm: Stockholm School of Economics and Stockholm Institute of Transition Economics.

Berkowitz, Dan, Katharina Pistor, and Jean-François Richard. 2003. "Economic Development, Legality, and the Transplant Effect." *European Economic Review* 47(1):165–95.

Besley, Timothy. 1995. "Property Rights and Investment Incentives: Theory and Evidence from Ghana." *Journal of Political Economy* 103(5):903–37.

Bhattacharya, Utpal, and Hazem Daouk. 2002. "The World Price of Insider Trading." *Journal of Finance* 57(1):75–108.

Black, Bernard. 2001. "The Corporate Governance Behavior and Market Value of Russian Firms." *Emerging Markets Review* 2(2):89–108.

Black, Bernard, and Reinier Kraakman. 1996. "A Self-Enforcing Model of Company Law." *Harvard Law Review* 109(8):1911–81.

Black, Bernard, Hasung Jang, and Woochan Kim. 2003. "Does Corporate Governance Affect Firms' Market Values? Evidence from Korea." Working Paper. Austin, Tex.: University of Texas School of Law. [http://ssrn.com/abstract=311275].

Broadman, Harry G. 1999. "Reducing Structural Dominance and Entry Barriers in Russian Industry, in Russian Enterprise Reform." World Bank Discussion Paper 400. Washington, D.C: World Bank.

Coffee, John C. Jr. 1999. "The Future as History: The Prospects for Global Convergence in Corporate Governance and its Implications." *Northwestern University Law Review* 93:641–707.

———. 2002. "Racing Towards the Top? The Impact of Cross-Listings and Stock Market Competition on International Corporate Governance." *Columbia Law Review* 102(7):1757–831.

Cooter, Robert D. 1991. "Economic Theories of Legal Liability." *Journal of Economic Perspectives* 5(3):11–30.

Defond, Mark L., and Mingyi Hung. 2003. "Investor Protection and Corporate Governance: Evidence from Worldwide CEO Turnover." Los Angeles, Calif.: University of Southern California, Leventhal School of Accounting.

Dixit, Avinash. 2004. *Lawlessness and Economics: Alternative Modes of Governance*. Princeton, N.J.: Princeton University Press.

Djankov, Simeon, Edward L. Glaeser, Rafael La Porta, Florencio López-de-Silanes, and Andrei Shleifer. 2002. "The Regulation of Entry." *Quarterly Journal of Economics* 117(1):1–37.

———. 2003. "The New Comparative Economics." *Journal of Comparative Economics* 31(4):595–619.

Durnev, A., and E.H. Kim. 2005. "To Steal or Not to Steal: Firm Attributes, Legal Environment, and Valuation." *Journal of Finance* 6(3):1461–93.

Dyck, Alexander, and Luigi Zingales. 2003. "The Corporate Governance Role of the Media." In R. Islam, ed., *The Right to Tell: The Role of the Media in Development*. Washington, D.C.: World Bank.

Ellickson, R.C. 1991. *Order Without Law*. Cambridge, Mass.: Harvard University Press.

Faccio, Mara, and Larry H.P. Lang. 2002. "The Ultimate Ownership of Western European Corporations." *Journal of Financial Economics* 65(3):365–95.

Gambetta, Diego. 1993. *The Sicilian Mafia: The Business of Private Protection*. Cambridge, Mass.: Harvard University Press.

Gibbons, Michael. 2002. "Is Corporate Governance Ineffective in Emerging Markets?" *Journal of Financial and Quantitative Analysis* 38(1):231–50.

Glaeser, Edward, and Andrei Shleifer. 2001. "A Reason for Quantity Regulation." *American Economic Review Papers and Proceedings* 91(2):431–35.

———. 2002. "Legal Origins." *Quarterly Journal of Economics* 117(4):1193–230.

Glaeser, Edward, Jose Sheinkman, and Andrei Shleifer. 2003. "Injustice of Inequality." *Journal of Monetary Economics*, Carnegie-Rochester Series on Public Policy 50(1):199–222.

Greif, Avner. 1992. "Institutions and International Trade: Lessons from the Commercial Revolution." *American Economic Review* 82(2):128–33.

———. 1993. "Contract Enforceability and Economic Institutions in Early Trade: The Maghribi Traders' Coalition." *American Economic Review* 83(3):525–84.

Guriev, Sergei, Olga Lazareva, Andrei Rachinsky, and Sergei Tsukhlo. 2003. "Corporate Governance in Russian Industry." CEFIR Working Paper. Moscow: Center for Economic and Financial Research.

Hauswald, Robert, and Ulrich Hege. 2003. "Ownership and Control in Joint Ventures: Theory and Evidence." CEPR Discussion Paper 4056. London: Centre for Economic Policy Research.

Hay, Jonathan R., Andrei Shleifer, and Robert Vishny. 1996. "Toward a Theory of Legal Reform." *European Economic Review* 40(3–5):559–67.

Immordino, Giovanni, and Marco Pagano. 2003. "Design and Enforcement of Legal Standards." CSEF Working Paper 98. Italy: Centre for Studies in Economics and Finance, University of Salerno.

Klapper, Leora F., and Inessa Love. 2003. "Corporate Governance, Investor Protection and Performance in Emerging Markets." *Journal of Corporate Finance* 10(5):703–28.

Laeven, Luc, and Christopher Woodruff. 2003. "The Quality of the Legal System, Firm Ownership, and Firm Size." Mimeo. Washington, D.C.: World Bank, Financial Sector Vice-Presidency.

La Porta, Rafael, Florencio Lopez-de-Silanes, and Andrei Shleifer. 1999. "Corporate Ownership Around the World." *Journal of Finance* 54(2):471–518.

———. 2006. "What Works in Securities Laws." *Journal of Finance* 61(1):1–32.

Licht, Amir. 2003. "Cross-Listing and Corporate Governance: Bonding or Avoiding?" *Chicago Journal of International Law* 4(1):141–63.

Lopez-de-Silanes, Florencio. 2004. "A Survey of Securities Laws and Enforcement." Working Paper 3405. Washington, D.C.: World Bank.

McMillan, John, and Christopher Woodruff. 1999. "Dispute Prevention Without Courts in Vietnam." *Journal of Law, Economics and Organization* 15(3):637–58.

Milhaupt, Curtis J. 2003. "Nonprofit Organizations as Investor Protection: Economic Theory, and Evidence from East Asia." Mimeo. New York: Weatherhead East Asian Institute, Columbia University.

Morck, Randall, and Bernard Yeung. 2003. "Corporate Governance and Family Control." Discussion Paper 1. Washington, D.C.: Global Corporate Governance Forum

North, Douglass C. 1991. *Institutions, Institutional Change, and Economic Performance.* Cambridge: Cambridge University Press.

Ostrom, Elinor, Roy Gardner, and James Walker. 1990. "The Nature of Common-Pool Resource Problems." *Rationality and Society* 2(3):335–58.

Pinheiro Castelar, Armand, and Celia Cabral. 2001. "Credit Markets in Brazil: The Role of Enforcement and Other Institutions." In Marco Pagano, ed., *Defusing Default.* Washington, D.C.: Inter-American Development Bank and OECD.

Pistor, Katharina, and Chenggang Xu. 2003. "Incomplete Law: A Conceptual and Analytical Framework and its Application to the Evolution of Financial Market Regulation." New York: Columbia University Law School.

Pistor, Katharina, Martin Raiser, and Stanislav Gelfer. 2000. "Law and Finance in Transition Econo-mies." *Economics of Transition* 8(2):325–68.

Polinsky, Mitchell, and Steven Shavell. 2000. "The Economic Theory of Public Enforcement of Law." *Journal of Economic Literature* 38(1):45–76.

Rossi, Stefano, and Paolo Volpin. 2003. "Cross-Country Determinants of Mergers and Acquisitions." CEPR Working Paper 3889. London: Centre for Economic Policy Research.

Shleifer, Andrei, and Robert Vishny. 1997. "A Survey of Corporate Governance." *Journal of Finance* 52(2):737–83.

Siegel, Jordan I. 2005. "Can Foreign Firms Bond Themselves Effectively by Renting U.S. Securities Laws?" *Journal of Financial Economics* 75(2):319–59.

Slinko, Irina, Yevgeny Yakovlev, and Ekaterina Zhuravskaya. 2002. "State Capture in the Russian Regions." CEFIR Working Paper. Moscow: Center for Economic and Financial Research.

Stulz, René, and Rohan Williamson. 2003. "Culture, Openness, and Finance." *Journal of Financial Economics* 70(3):313–49.

Zhuravskaya, Ekaterina, and Oleg Zamulin. 2003. "Administrative Barriers to Small Business in Russia: Results from a New Survey." CEFIR Working Paper. Moscow: Center for Economic and Financial Research.